BRIDGE IS A CONVERSATION

To all my friends of the bridge world, with my best wishes for many slams . . . and making them!

—Gerard

CONTENTS

INTRODUCTION

I have played bridge for more than sixty years now, first learning the game from my mother, then learning it by playing party bridge with my parents and my younger brother, then with my parents and their friends, then with their friends and strangers, then in duplicate clubs in France, Israel, and England, and now, happily, in the United States. I learned from all these experiences different systems or methods, a huge number of conventions, how to bid and misbid, how to understand and get confused, how to make impossible contracts, and how to blow cold ones.

Like everybody else, I have fumed at my partner for misunderstanding a bid I thought was clear, blamed my partner for the wrong contract, or thrown an easy one. How many times? I won't tell!

But now, a bit older and maybe a bit wiser, I have been trying to find the reasons for all these years of errors, misunderstandings, and miscommunications. I have come up with the concept that playing bridge does not consist of playing a system, but that bridge is a *conversation*, in which the system is the communicative language.

Playing mostly with experts in recent years, I have noticed that all, knowingly or not, use that concept.

I have tried to find writings on the subject, but in vain, so I decided to compile my observations and thoughts and present my own theories.

My purpose here is not to teach how bridge systems are built, nor to describe their content, but rather to clarify how to use them the way the best players in the world use them and to offer an alternative to simply "playing by the book." You will find the game much more interesting, challenging, and enjoyable than you ever dreamed it could be.

In the pages that follow, I will also demonstrate how the principles I put forward are valid regardless of the bidding system used.

CHAPTER 1

The Basic Principle of Bridge Conversation

When two people want to establish and maintain communication with each other, they use a language that both can understand and manipulate, such as English, Chinese, Hebrew, or body language.

Even "body language"? Yes! When I was at school and had an urgent need during a class, I had to raise my hand and wait for the teacher to respond to it. One single arm signal from him was enough to make me jump out of my seat and dash out of the classroom.

The interesting part of this short story is that the teacher was able to have two conversations at the same time, in two different languages. He conducted the class in French and communicated with me in body language, and neither of the conversations interrupted the other one.

Each one of these languages has vocabulary, grammar, and syntax—even body language.

We do the same thing when we play bridge. We may have a casual conversation with the other players around the table in English or Turkish or Japanese while simultaneously exchanging bridge information in the language of bridge. Bridge is a language, too!

The Vocabulary

In all spoken languages, the vocabulary consists of a collection of words used to describe a physical object, a concept, or a feeling (nouns); an action (verbs); or to describe or modify something (adjectives and adverbs). Other words do not have any specific meaning but are used as language hinges (articles and pronouns).

It is important to realize that each descriptive word in a vocabulary is only a sound, even when it is written down on paper. For instance, the word *horse*, in itself, does not have a meaning. Whoever invented the English language decided that *horse* would be the word associated with the four-legged animal that makes a funny noise when it tries to talk. That meaning has stuck, and today, anybody who speaks English knows what a horse is.

"To horse around," having "horse sense," and other expressions built on the word horse derive from the concept of horse.

This was a simple example. Some of the words in the vocabulary may have several different meanings altogether, depending on the context in which they are used. For instance, the word *fan* represents an object used to cool oneself off when the temperature is too high. When a performer gets on stage and his/her fans are in the audience, it can get hot. That's something else altogether.

The English language has the biggest vocabulary, with around 250,000 words; French, around 150,000; Spanish, 120,000, etc. A standard English dictionary commonly defines 50,000 of them, but few people actually recognize half of that number, and most do not use more than 5,000.

In highly sophisticated languages with a vast array of words, like English, most words have one or a limited number of different meanings. Therefore, each word is less dependant on the context in which it is used. In more compact languages, most words depend entirely on their context, as we will see later on when exploring the language of bridge, which vocabulary contains only forty words.

One does not need to know every single word in the English dictionary in order to communicate in that language. That would be a lifetime commitment, but in bridge, novices learn the complete list of bridge words right away.

In any language, vocabulary, grammar, and syntax are the tools that permit a structured and intelligible conversation.

The Grammar

The grammar is the set of rules that governs the classification of the words into language constituents, expressions, propositions, sentences, paragraphs, etc. The meaning of each language constituent is a function of the relative position of each word used.

In English, "to go around a horse" and "to go horse around" have different meanings because, in accordance to the grammar rules, the order in which the words are placed determines the class of each one. In our example, the word *horse* can be a noun or a verb, depending on its position relative to the other words in the sentence.

The English language is particularly notorious for the simplicity of its grammar. The English vocabulary is so extensive that grammar does not need to be very complex in order to express just about anything one might want to say. The game of bridge is just the opposite, with its very limited vocabulary; therefore, it needs a very complex grammar.

In bridge, *auctions* are language constituents, and each bid in the auction varies according to its position. This whole book reviews this in detail. Good bidders learn to arrange the words with sound grammar they learned from bridge writers like Culbertson, Goren, and others. These bridge writers all were, or are, masters at teaching it.

Experts use the same words, of course, but with advanced grammar. Some, like Edwin Kantar, Mike Lawrence, Max Hardy, and others, are excellent teachers of advanced grammar.

The Syntax

The syntax is the set of rules organizing the language constituents into sentences.

In English, "to go around a horse" is an acceptable syntax, while "around a horse to go" is not.

In bridge, doubling an opponent's bid is an acceptable syntax, while doubling a partner's bid is not.

Learning the syntax of a language, whether English, Chinese, or any other language, is a must. Lack of knowledge of syntax is often considered to be the same as a lack of education; isn't that true?

The bridge syntax, just like the bridge vocabulary, is something novices learn right away.

The Gerard Principle

Yes, the bridge language is no exception. It has its own vocabulary, grammar, and syntax, and in order to play bridge one needs to know all of them.

Participants in the conversation must also follow a specific protocol. All cannot talk at the same time. Some people ask questions, and there are times for that. Others answer, and there are times for that. Some make statements, and there are times for that, too—and this is only the tip of the iceberg. There is a right time and a wrong time for everything.

As in any communication between people, people and machines, or machines and machines, there needs to be a protocol and, so far, no one has identified bridge's mysterious communication protocol. All great players, teachers, and super-experts use it every time they bid, but none has articulated it.

Call it what you want, the Gerard Principle or some other name, but it governs all bridge conversations. That is what this book is about.

CHAPTER 2

The Object of Conversations

Some people talk for no reason. They don't have anything specific to say, but they say it anyway. They hope to grab someone's attention and start a conversation. The reason is that they want to feel that they are "somebody." I'll leave it to psychologists to analyze their deep motivations. The bottom line is that, even for these people, there is a reason and a goal for trying to communicate.

There is always a goal for conversations, and that is to either inform or request information.

Bridge is no exception to the rule. For each team, the goal of the conversation between partners is to find an eight-card fit to play the contract in (or settle on a NT—short for No Trump—contract if no fit can be found) at a level that will bring the maximum number of scoring points possible. This is done by one player passing information to the other player, and the other player processing the information and making a determination of what to ask next or what to do next.

Both teams carry a conversation, and often enough each team tries to derail the other team's conversation. It is part of the competition process that takes place in the game. The proof that it is a competition is that, even in social games, after a board has been played, the score is kept. At the end of the game, there is a winner and a loser.

Both teams engage, one board at a time, in an intellectual confrontation, at the end of which one will have the pleasure of playing the contract and the other one the misfortune of having to defend it.

During the search for a contract to play, one team, usually the one with more points, is the offense; the other one is the defense. The team on the defensive will try to put a wrench into the spokes and prevent the team on the offensive from getting it right.

Without competition, and with hands that are fairly standard, a team formed of decent players can find the right contract. It's like driving in a straight line on a freeway with no other cars around. You press on the accelerator, and off you go. You make a few bids and find a contract. All you have to do now is make it.

But many times, the opponents won't let it happen so easily. They will interfere in the bidding. The road is not a straight line on a freeway anymore, but a racing track with many turns, chicanes, narrow passages, and all sorts of other traps. You know how to drive, but the other guys are good. That's when you really need an in-depth knowledge of how to use the tools.

Bridge is a mind game, but not between partners. It is a mind game between opposing teams. Whatever goes on between partners during the game is meant to benefit the team in the match, and the result depends very much on how well the communication has worked between the two of them.

The communication between partners needs to be precise and efficient in order for them to achieve good results.

CHAPTER 3

The Bridge Language Elements

In bridge, the vocabulary is limited to forty words altogether:

1♣	1♦	1♥	1♠	1NT
2♣	2♦	2♥	2♠	2NT
3♣	3♦	3♥	3♠	3NT
4♣	4♦	4♥	4♠	4NT
5♣	5♦	5♥	5♠	5NT
6♣	6♦	6♥	6♠	6NT
7♣	7♦	7♥	7♠	7NT
Pass	Dbl	RDbl	Alert	Skip

Table 3-1

The words *alert* and *skip* are informative only. *Alert* is meant as a warning to the opposite team that a bid has a meaning other than the standard meaning, and *skip* announces an abnormal flow in the auction, caused by skipping levels.

The grammar is the protocol used to play the game, also called the rules of the game. One of the rules is that players bid by auction using exclusively the forty terms listed in the table above, each term in the list being either one bid or a warning.

The lowest bid in an auction is 1♣ and the highest is 7NT RDbl.

I assume that if you are reading this work, you already have been playing bridge for a while and are familiar with most rules and particularly with the concept of bridge auctions.

People from different origins, backgrounds, and native languages can still play bridge together, provided they know the bridge vocabulary and follow the rules of the game.

What do all these words, like 1♣, 2♥, 4♠, etc., mean?

By themselves, they do not mean anything. For each of them to be meaningful, you need to agree with your partner on the significance of it. Once this is done, for the duration of your agreement, the meaning will always be the same.

For example, you might decide that a 1♣ opening bid will show 13-21 points with three or more clubs, deny any major by five cards with more than three clubs or fewer diamonds than clubs, or you might decide that 1♣ opening bid means that you have 16 or more points with any shape or again, you might decide that 1♣ has some other meaning.

As mentioned earlier, the bridge vocabulary is very limited in size, and each word has multiple meanings, depending on what other bids preceded it.

For example, in SAYC (Standard American Yellow Card) system, 1NT may mean different things, depending on the context in which that bid is placed, as shown in Example 3-1 through Example 3-10.

North	East	South	West	
1NT				Shows a balanced hand with 15-17 High Card Points

Example 3-1

North	East	South	West	
1♣	1NT			Shows a balanced hand with 15-18 High Card Points

Example 3-2

North	East	South	West	Implies a balanced hand with 6-9 High Card Points, neither a four-card major nor a five-club support
1♣	*Pass*	1NT		

Example 3-3

North	East	South	West	Implies a hand with 6-9 High Card Points, neither four spades nor five-club support, but with a stopper in hearts
1♣	*1♥*	1NT		

Example 3-4

North	East	South	West	Implies 11-14 High Card Points, a balanced hand, and a club stopper
1♣	*Pass*	**Pass**	*1NT*	

Example 3-5

North	East	South	West	Implies a balanced hand with a minimum of 6 points, less than three diamonds, less than four cards in either major, but a club stopper
1♣	*1♦*	**Pass**	*1NT*	

Example 3-6

North	East	South	West	Implies a balanced hand with a minimum of 9 points and four cards in the unbid suits.
1♣	*Pass*	**1♥**	*1NT*	

Example 3-7

North	East	South	West	Implies a balanced hand with a minimum of 6 points, less than three diamonds, less than four spades, but with stoppers in both hearts and clubs
1♣	*1♦*	**1♥**	*1NT*	

Example 3-8

North	East	South	West	Shows a balanced hand with 12-17 High Card Points, denies four-card heart support, denies four spades and denies six clubs
1♣	*Pass*	1♥	*Pass*	
1NT				

Example 3-9

North	East	South	West	Shows 6-9 High Card Points, denies four-spade support and denies five-club support
1♣	*Pass*	1♥	*Pass*	
1♠	*Pass*	1NT		

Example 3-10

As shown above, the word 1NT does not always mean the same thing. It is very dependant on the context in which it is used.

Notice that in the ten examples above, sometimes the word *shows* is used and sometimes the word *implies* is used. This is neither accidental nor arbitrary.

In a later chapter, there will be a full explanation of what the difference is, but for the time being, let's just state that *shows* stands for mandatory meaning while *implies* stands for less stringently defined meaning.

The word 1NT is only one word. Every word, from 1♣ up to 7♠, has several meanings depending on the context. Only 7NT has a single meaning, since it is the highest possible bid.

Even the words Pass, Dbl, and RDbl have several meanings, depending on where they are used in any given auction.

Gerard Cohen

Gerard's Tidbit of the Night: Bridge History

The word bridge *comes from the Russian "biritch," meaning announcer. Bridge players announce their contract bids. Harold Vanderbilt created the game in 1925, during a shipboard cruise, and Ely Culbertson released the first bridge treaty, called the* Blue Book, *which topped all book sales for the year 1931.*

CHAPTER 4

Using Bridge Systems

It would literally take days, weeks, months, or maybe years to define the meanings of each and every bid whenever you got a new partner, and it would therefore be impossible to play.

I often play bridge on the Internet. If I had to define the meaning of every single bid before starting to play with a specific partner, my telephone bill would be astronomical. Luckily, others have done that already; the use of a preset of meanings is highly recommended. This is what a bidding system is: a preset of meanings for each and every bid, depending on its context within an auction.

Early bidding systems were very skimpy, and all bids had a natural meaning. If you opened with 2♣, it showed a strong hand with a club suit, while 2♦ showed a strong hand with a diamond suit, etc.

With time, more sophisticated bidding systems appeared, incorporating more and more artificial bids and representing specific and recurring point counts and card distributions. The idea was, and still is, to have bidding systems that allow players to communicate the content of their hand with increased precision.

New bidding systems pop up each day, devised by highly competent bridge players throughout the world. Some of them become very famous, while others remain unknown to most. Some of the systems are more complex than others.

For ease of recognition, each one of these bidding systems is given a name, tentatively unique to that system. Among the most famous systems are Standard American and its yellow card variation (SAYC), Two over One Game Force (2/1GF), Precision, Blue Team Club, Acol, Roman Club, Albaran Method, and many more. More recently, Polish Club, Nightmare by Buratti and Lanzarotti, and others have appeared.

Why so many of them? It is because none of them has yet reached the state of perfection. They all have limitations, though their scope has improved, thanks to constant modifications. They may even get a new name or a modified name that encapsulates the new adjunctions, deletions, and modifications. Recently, I played Roman Club 1959 with a partner and got rimmed by him, because I used a modification that appeared in the 1961 version. It's much like trying to put a replacement part for a certain model car in another year of that model. It does not always work.

It is impossible to say which system is better. Each one of them has its merits and its downfalls. All have in common that they attempt to define the hand being held with the greatest precision possible. It seems obvious, to me at least, that the more complex the system, the greater the precision; but it is also more difficult to memorize the bidding procedure, and therefore, the chance is higher of making errors during auctions.

One thing is certain, however. No bidding system is perfect, because no bidding system can cover the seemingly infinite number of combinations of cards held by players around a bridge table.

Most people select their bidding system to conform to the bridge community around them. If only one system is used, they are kind of stuck playing that one system, but most often, two, three, or more systems are played, and the choice depends on other factors, like the amount of time they wish to spend on learning a system, how often they play, or how many other players they know who use it. On top of that, players need to make an honest assessment of their retention capabilities.

It is of no use for someone who only plays party bridge once a month with the neighbors and who only knows Goren's 5 Cards Major System (and partially at that), to learn the Italian Blue Team Club System.

CHAPTER 5

Using Conventions

Some bids have a simple meaning, their source is the bidding system used, and they describe succinctly the content of the hand in points and promise cards in the named suit. We shall refer to them as natural bids. For instance, in the SAYC system, the opening bid of 1♠ shows a hand of 13-21 points with five spades or more.

Some bids, also originated by the bidding system used, do not represent that the hand contains any specific cards in the named suit but do give other information about the hand. We will refer to these either as artificial bids or as conventional calls. The most famous one in the SAYC system is the opening bid of 2♣, which shows a minimum of 22 HCPs (High Cards Points) or eight and a half quick tricks but does not imply the presence of clubs at all.

Finally, on top of the bidding system you opt for, other subsystems can be integrated. These are called conventions. Some simple ones actually are very similar to a conventional call, in the sense that the whole convention consists of one single artificial bid. Others, more complex, start with an artificial bid, continue with relays and questions, and eventually exit back to the original system.

An example of a simple convention is the Michaels Convention, in which cue bidding an opening of a minor suit shows both majors by five cards.

The most famous of any complex convention is probably the one that appeared in 1945, as an article written by Samuel Stayman in the *Bridge World Magazine*, which publicized a new convention devised by his longtime partner, George Rapee. It has since revolutionized the world of bridge. The convention became known as the Stayman Convention, even though Stayman himself refused over and over to take the credit for its invention.

Conventions are usually given a specific name, just as systems have names. Just to mention a few, Ghestem, Stayman, Blackwood, Jacoby 2NT, Bergen Raises, Lebensohl, Drury, and several hundred more, are part of a list that gets longer every day. Some of them made the Hall of Fame, while others remain less popular.

CHAPTER 6

Using Partnership Agreements

Some conventions are so intimate to a partnership that nobody else besides two partners knows of it or uses it. These are not even called conventions but merely partnership agreements. They don't usually have a name and must be used with caution. Some of them may actually be illegal to use in a bridge club, because they do not meet the criteria imposed by the local bridge authorities, like the ACBL in the United States, the FFB in France, etc.

I recently played on the Internet against a pair that opened 1♥ to show five spades and a four-card minor with a point count of 7-13. This is a typical case of a partnership agreement that does not conform to the rules of the ACBL, except in some Flight A tournaments, perhaps.

Technically, partnership agreements and conventions look alike. Everything I have said about conventions is also true of partnership agreements.

As these partnership agreements become better known, they may even become conventions, recognized by national and international bridge organizations.

At any rate, these are the tools you work with when you play bridge. The question now is: How do you use these tools?

Gerard's Tidbit of the Night: Bridge History

When Mr. Easley Blackwood submitted his famous Blackwood Convention in 1935, it was rejected. Here is a copy of the response by the Bridge World Magazine, *the authority on the game of bridge at the time:*

THE BRIDGE WORLD
May 24, 1935

Mr. R. E. Blackwood
Room 1411
11 South Meridian St.,
Indianapolis, Ind.

Dear Mr. Blackwood!

We read your article with interest and enjoyment, but we fear that we cannot use it in the *Bridge World*.

While the suggestion is a good one, the four-no-trump bid will remain informative rather than an interrogative bid, and our subscribers are too prone to accept anything printed in the *Bridge World* as a recommended change in the Culbertson System, unless it is specifically part of another known system.

We hope that you will at some time submit another manuscript to us for, judging by the merit of this one, we are sure that we can make use of it.

> Yours sincerely,
> The Bridge World
>
> Albert H. Morehead
> Editor

In 1949, fourteen years later, the convention had been mentioned in fifty-seven books and translated into seventeen languages.

CHAPTER 7

Format of a Conversation in Bridge

Conversations in bridge, as you already know, are done in an auction format.

A bridge auction is the process by which two teams compete for the right of playing a bridge contract. Before the end of an auction, one team has to forfeit that right, and the other wins it. The highest bidder is the one who wins the auction, even if he/she did not intend to win it—but that is another story.

For an auction to exist, at least one of the teams has to enter it by making a bid. If both teams shy away from making a bid other than Pass, there is no auction, and the hand will not be played. Usually at least one team, if not both, will enter the auction.

During auctions, both teams make bids, the meaning of which comes from the selected bidding system itself, from some convention, or from a partnership agreement that they are using. The selection of the bids depends on the kind of information each player wants to transmit to his/her partner.

Each team may use its own set of bidding system, conventions, and partnership agreements, but if a team's bid has a different meaning from what the other team uses, this must be advised and explained to the other team.

As an auction progresses, its level keeps increasing, and so does the risk of overshooting the level of the right contract.

Bridge is not a game of poker, though. Making bids randomly and lying about the points and shape content of one's hand to make the other team go astray usually leads to very poor results.

The general idea is that one team attempts to win the right to play a contract, while the other tries to either steal that right or to interfere with the first team in such a manner that the first team does not have enough room left in the auction to communicate all the information it needs before deciding in what suit and at what level the hand will be played.

It is important to realize that all bidding systems, conventions, and partnership agreements are only tools used to communicate the hands being held, in points and shape, between team partners during auctions. They are not the essence of bridge. The essence of bridge is to find the best possible contract and to beat the opponents. Good judgment, precise timing, competitive spirit, and other elements are other important factors in the making of a good bridge game.

Bridge is not a game played "by the book." The book is used to play the game of bridge.

Using the book, players discover what their partner holds, by asking questions and/or communicating their own holdings. Once the discovery is completed, they decide what they wish to do with their hands. All this is done in a conversational form, using the bridge language for it.

CHAPTER 8

Components of Conversation

Each team carries its own conversation, in competition with the other team.

There are three main components to conversations in any language:

- making statements
- asking questions
- answering questions

In our everyday communication with others, we may start conversations with either a statement or with a question, depending on the reason why we start it.

For instance, we may it start with:

- a statement, like "I am thirsty. I need a drink." That can be followed by a question, like "What would you like to drink?" (to which the answer is one element of a list, like mineral water, milk, coffee, tea, wine, or hard liquor, just to name a few);
- a question requesting an inventory list answer, like "What do you have that I can drink?" (to which the answer might be "I have mineral water, milk, coffee, tea, wine, hard liquor); or

- a question requesting a yes/no answer, like "Do you have something to drink?" (to which the answer is "Yes, I do" or "No, I don't").

To questions, one responds with answers; to statements, one may either ask questions in order to get more details, or accept the statement for what it is and not reply at all.

In fact, when a conversation starts with a question, it implies a statement even if the statement was not enounced. The question "Do you have something to drink?" usually implies that the person who asks it is thirsty and needs a drink.

In the example above, the conversation is oriented toward quenching somebody's thirst, but there are an infinite number of objects for conversations. It is therefore necessary to let the other person know what the conversation will be about, either by starting with a statement or by asking a question that implies its objective.

If you start with a question like "Do you have one?" I defy the person you ask the question of to know what you are talking about.

Bridge is no different, but conversations in bridge are more structured because they follow an auction format, and only a limited number of bids are available per player, while casual conversations in other languages are usually freestyle.

In the upcoming chapters, we will review that structure in great detail, but before starting, let's subcategorize statements into 1) opening statements, statements that start the conversation and 2) closing statements, statements that normally close the conversation.

Let's also subdivide questions into (1) inventorial questions, questions that require an answer extracted from an inventory of available bids, which I will call *questions*, and (2) invitational questions, questions that request a pass if the answer is no and anything else if the answer is yes, which I'll call *invitations*.

According to these subdivisions, the components of bridge are the following:

- making opening statements
- asking questions
- making invitations
- answering questions
- responding to invitations
- making closing statements

When an invitation is refused, it may mark the end of the conversation. In this case, an invitation has the same effect as a closing statement.

From this list of components, we can dress up four basic auction models, depending on how the auctions end, either with a closing statement or with an invitation.

For ease of comprehension, we will assume for the time being that only the North/South team is entering the auction.

Also, since the number of questions is variable, we will replace Question 1 to North with Questions.

North	East	South	West
Opening statement	*Pass*	**Questions**	***Pass***
Answers	*Pass*	**Pass**	Pass

Model 8-1

Where pass by South is converting the last answer by North into the contract to be played:

North	East	South	West
Opening statement	*Pass*	**Questions**	*Pass*
Answers	*Pass*	**Invitation**	*Pass*
Pass	*Pass*		

Model 8-2

Where the invitation by South of playing at the next level contract is refused by North because of lack of extra values:

North	East	South	West
Opening statement	*Pass*	**Questions**	*Pass*
Answers	*Pass*	**Invitation**	*Pass*
Accept invitation	*Pass*	**Pass**	*Pass*

Model 8-3

Where the invitation by South of playing at the next level contract is accepted by North:

North	East	South	West
Opening statement	*Pass*	**Questions**	*Pass*
Answers	*Pass*	**Closing statement**	*Pass*
Pass	*Pass*		

Model 8-4

Where North accepts the closing statement by South:

If North has extra values that South is not aware of, North is entitled to reopen the conversation, and one of the four models is used again but without new opening statement, for instance in

North	East	South	West
Opening statement	*Pass*	**Questions**	*Pass*
Answers	*Pass*	**Closing statement**	*Pass*
Questions	*Pass*	Answers	*Pass*
Closing statement	*Pass*	Pass	*Pass*

Model 8-5

The conversation ends only when three passes in a row are performed.

Each time a question is asked, it is performed as an auction bid. The more complex the conversation is, the higher the auction climbs. It is therefore necessary to consider that asking too many questions may overshoot the auction level, after which no contract can make any more.

Technically, the only limitation is the number of bids available before one hits the ceiling of 7NT RDbl, beyond which no auction can go.

Let's show here four examples, each one using another type of closing statement. All examples are auctions made using the SAYC bidding system.

In all examples, the auction starts the same way:

North	East	South	West
1♠	*Pass*	2♣	*Pass*
2♥	*Pass*	**Bid?**	

Example 8-1

Where 1♠ by North is an opening statement meaning "I have an opening hand and a natural spade suit";

A 2♣ by South is a question to North asking for further description of the hand;

A 2♥ by North is the answer to South's question that describes a hand having a second suit in hearts and a bare opening.

- Discouraging closing statement:

North	East	South	West
1♠	*Pass*	2♣	*Pass*
2♥	*Pass*	**Pass**	*Pass*

Example 8-1A

Pass by South is a closing statement that means "Whatever happens from here on in the auction, do not bid again, unless you did not tell me the whole story." In other words, even if East/West decides to place a bid after the Pass bid by South, North is strongly advised not to bid again.

Notice that in the absence of a bid by West after South has passed, North does not even have a chance to bid again. When South passes, he/she must therefore keep in mind that North may not be able to bid again before passing. South is not to prejudge what West might do. I have myself been caught many times in that situation, maybe not in such a simple auction, but in auctions where it seemed evident to me that West would rebid but did not, leaving me hanging with a partial contract when game should have been reached.

- Invitation and negative answer:

North	East	South	West
1♠	*Pass*	2♣	*Pass*
2♥	*Pass*	3♥	*Pass*
Pass	*Pass*		

Example 8-1B

The 3♥ by South is an invitation that means "I propose to play a heart contract at the game level, unless you do not have extra values, in which case, you should accept the contract at the current level."

Pass by North is the acceptance of South's proposal to play the contract in 3♥ and a denial that it has the extra values needed to reach game level.

- Invitation and positive answer:

With the maximum value in the opening range, 15 or 16 points in North hand, the auction would have ended thus:

North	East	South	West
1♠	*Pass*	2♣	*Pass*
2♥	*Pass*	3♥	*Pass*
4♥	*Pass*	**Pass**	*Pass*

Example 8-1C

Notice that in this case, North is not given the choice of the suit to play the contract in, but only the level at which to play the heart contract.

- Proposing closing statement:

North	East	South	West
1♠	*Pass*	2♣	*Pass*
2♥	*Pass*	**3NT**	*Pass*
Pass	*Pass*		

Example 8-1D

The 3NT by South is a closing statement that means "I propose to play NT at the game level, if it's okay with you, partner." It implies that South has enough points and enough diamonds to justify that decision.

Pass by North is the acceptance of South's proposal to play the contract in 3NT.

North might refuse 3NT in Example 8-1D with a hand having 15 points and a distribution that could make him/her believe that slam is a good possibility. He/she could then inquire about how many aces, and maybe even kings, are in South's hand, using the Gerber Convention, as shown here:

North	East	South	West
1♠	*Pass*	2♣	*Pass*
2♥	*Pass*	3NT	*Pass*
4♣	*Pass*	4♠	*Pass*
5♣	*Pass*	5♥	*Pass*
6NT	*Pass*	**Pass**	*Pass*

Example 8-1E

Where 4♣ by North is a conventional reopening question meaning "How many aces do you have?"

The 4♠ by South is the conventional response to North showing two aces,

The 5♣ by North is the conventional question to ask South "How many kings do you have?"

The 5♥ is the conventional response by South to North showing 1 king,

The 6NT by North is a closing statement that means "Based on your answers, let's play a small slam in NT."

Pass by South is the acceptance of North proposal.

Now, if North miscalculated his/her shot or made too many assumptions about South's hand, this contract might be too high, but South has no way to revert the auction. If South thinks that North went too high, his/her best bet is simply to accept the 6NT contract and bite the bullet.

Preacceptance may also be part of the answer to a question. A very useful example here demonstrates just that, in the American Standard System:

North	East	South	West
1NT	*Pass*	2♥	*Pass*
3♠	*Pass*	4♠	*Pass*
Pass	*Pass*		

Example 8-2

The 1NT by North is a statement that shows a 15-17-point balanced hand.

The 2♥ is a question by South asking North to bid spade.

The 3♠ is the response by North to South. It goes a bit further than simply responding. It gives South an extra piece of information. North hand has exactly 17 points and four spades in support, the maximum possible hand for the 1NT opening. The object is to encourage the partner to bid game in spades with a point count of 7 or 8.

The 4♠ is the closing statement by South fixing the contract at that level. When making this bid, South has a very precise idea of the values in North hand, making his/her decision much easier.

Not only one side has the privilege of bidding; we know that. An expanded and more realistic model would show that the conversation process is the same for both teams. When both teams enter the auction, the auction climbs up much faster than if only one team does all the bidding while the other keeps passing.

CHAPTER 9

Starting the Auctions

There is always a complete first round of auction. In other words, each player has to make at least one bid before any given auction closes.

Sometimes no question is being asked, but there is always an opening statement and a closing statement by each side.

Model 8-4 is just reduced to this sequence:

North	East	South	West
Opening statement	*Pass*	**Closing statement**	***Pass***

Table 9-1

It is the simplest auction:

North	East	South	West
Pass	*Pass*	**Pass**	***Pass***

Example 9-1

North opening statement is: "My hand is too weak to enter the auction."

East opening statement is: "My hand is also too weak to enter the auction."

South closing statement is: "I have no question to ask. Let's not enter the auction."

West closing statement is: "I have no question either, so let's not start anything."

The hand is a passed out, and no score will be recorded for it.

Here's a slightly more complex auction:

North	East	South	West
1♥	*Pass*	Pass	*Pass*

Example 9-2

North opening statement is: "I have an opening hand and a natural heart suit."

East opening statement is: "I do not have anything to compete with."

South closing statement is: "I don't have enough values in my hand to ask any questions. Let's play 1♥ as our contract."

West closing statement is: "I don't have much either. Let's not compete."

This hand will play in a 1♥ contract.

In both cases, the auction ends after all four players have made a bid and no question was asked by any player; therefore, no answer was made, either.

These were two extreme cases, but most of the time the auctions go beyond the first round of bidding. It suffices to say that any player besides the dealer makes a bid, as in the example below:

North	East	South	West
1♥	*1NT*	Pass	*Pass*
Pass			

Example 9-3

In this auction, North has a chance at overriding South's decision not to compete, since there must be three passes after the last positive bid, and East has made a bid other than Pass. The only reason for North to rebid can be that the 1♥ opening statement does not reflect the true value of the hand, and North asks South to reconsider. In this instance, the conversation is relaunched by North.

As you can see, there is a great similarity between bridge auctions and a conversation in any other language.

Bridge players are people of few words. It is not because of their nature but because of the limited number of bids they can make in any given auction. The efficiency of their auctions depends greatly on how organized they are in conducting their conversation. The goal is to compete with the opponents in finding the best possible contract to play.

In the next chapters, we will deal with that organization.

Gerard Tidbit of the Night: Bridge and Health

An article published in a daily newspaper in late October 2001 said that bridge players live longer then non-bridge players. It may be true, but judging by the color of my hair, they also get old earlier than non-bridge players.

CHAPTER 10

The Opening Statements

A conversation between partners in bridge always starts with a statement that means one of the following:

- I have no values in my hand.
- I have some point values and no long suit.
- I have some point values and one long suit.
- I have some point values and more than one long suit.
- I have a huge hand that I cannot describe with a single statement.

Each team makes one, and only one, opening statement in any given auction:

North	East	South	West
Opening statement	*Opening statement*		

Model Extract 10-1

Both sides begin a bridge auction with an opening statement. In other words, the players in first and second seats each make an opening statement.

Opening Statement by the Player in First Seat

The player in the first seat, the dealer, who may hold from 0-37 points and zero to thirteen cards of any suit, makes the statement that he or she has nothing, has a somewhat valuable hand, has a strong hand, or has a hand with an unusual distribution.

The first bid made by the player in the first seat (the dealer) can only be an opening statement, which depends primarily on the point range and the shape of the hand.

Here are some charts of point ranges used for opening statements in four of the most common bidding systems.

SAYC active opening statements			
0 1 2 3 4	5 6 7 8 9 10 11	12 13 14 15 16 17 18 19 20 21	22+
Not to open with	Weak opening	Standard opening	Strong opening

Chart 10-1

2/1GF active opening statements			
0 1 2 3 4	5 6 7 8 9 10 11	12 13 14 15 16 17 18 19 20 21	22+
Not to open with	Weak opening	Standard opening	Strong opening

Chart 10-2

Precision active opening statements			
0 1 2 3 4	5 6 7 8 9 10	11 12 13 14 15	16+
Not to open with	Weak opening	Standard opening	Strong opening

Chart 10-3

Italian Blue Club active opening statements			
0 1 2 3 4 5 6	7 8 9 10 11	12 13 14 15 16	17+
Not to open with	Weak opening	Standard opening	Strong opening

Chart 10-4

The charts show a great variety of point ranges, with each bidding system having its own set.

Other systems may have other ranges, but they all have in common four specific ranges, and they are

- not-to-open-with range;
- weak opening range;
- intermediate opening range; and
- strong opening range.

Opening statements may only be one of the following types, depending primarily on the point range the hand belongs to and then on its shape.

Pass: A **passive opening statement** that shows a hand too weak in points and in shape to entice the partner into getting involved in a conversation and finding a contract.

An intermediate opening bid: A **natural active opening statement** that shows a hand with a specific point range and reflects the shape of the hand by naming the long suit or NT if there is no long suit.

A weak or preemptive bid: A **weak active opening statement** that shows a hand weaker in points than what is needed for an intermediate opening bid but extra length in the named suit. Such a bid is a warning to the partner that unless he or she is forced to bid again, the opener will not make any other bid in the auction.

An artificial bid: An **artificial active opening statement** that shows a hand of any value above the not-to-open range and/or any shape but without defining what specifically. In most bidding systems, and certainly in all recent ones, strong opening ranges are shown with an artificial active opening statement. The named suit does not reflect the specific holding of the hand in that suit and requires the partner to ask further questions in order to divulge this information.

Regardless of the bidding system used, this list can be charted with the actual points specifically required by that bidding system, as below:

Most modern bidding systems opening statements based on points			
Not to open with	Weak opening	Standard opening	Strong opening
Passive opening statement	Weak opening statement	Natural active opening statement	Artificial active opening statement

Chart 10-5

Artificial active opening statements are made with hands having an extraordinary distribution of suits, usually with more than one long suit, and have more than the not-to-open-with point range as defined by the bidding system used.

Most modern bidding systems opening statements based on points			
Not to open with	Weak opening	Standard opening	Strong opening
Passive opening statement	Artificial active opening statement		

Chart 10-6

In some very sophisticated systems, like Precision, point count is all that matters for the opening statement, because the distribution factor is dealt with in a very precise and specific way after the opening statement is made. For other systems, like SAYC or 2/1GF, there is some flexibility concerning the estimation of the point value of the hand when making the opening statement.

It is somewhat evident that a hand with a specific point range and a six-card suit is more valuable than a hand with the same point count but only a five-card suit. The value is even greater with a seven-card suit, etc.

By lowering by one point for each card held above the fifth one in any suit held, the requirements for each category of opening statements varies, as shown in the following opening chart of opening statements based on points:

SAYC active opening statements																						
0	1	2	3	4	5	6	7	8	9	10	11	12	13	14	15	16	17	18	19	20	21	22+
Not to open with		Weak opening										Standard opening with five cards									Strong opening	
			Weak opening										Standard opening with six cards							Strong opening		
				Weak opening							Standard opening with seven cards								Strong opening			
					Weak opening					Standard opening with eight cards							Strong opening					
						Weak opening				Standard opening with nine cards							Strong opening					
0	1	2	3	4	5	6	7	8	9	10	11	12	13	14	15	16	17	18	19	20	21	22+

Table 10-1

For the 2/1GF system, a very similar chart can be drawn, but the scale starts at 12 points; therefore, all ranges are shifted by one point to the left.

2/1GF active opening statements																						
0	1	2	3	4	5	6	7	8	9	10	11	12	13	14	15	16	17	18	19	20	21	22+
Not to open with		Weak opening									Standard opening with five cards										Strong opening	
			Weak opening							Standard opening with six cards									Strong opening			
				Weak opening			Standard opening with seven cards										Strong opening					
					Weak opening				Standard opening with eight cards							Strong opening						
						Weak opening			Standard opening with nine cards							Strong opening						
0	1	2	3	4	5	6	7	8	9	10	11	12	13	14	15	16	17	18	19	20	21	22+

Table 10-2

In modern bridge, more and more players use this advanced method to determine the range a hand belongs to before making an active opening bid.

Again, this is not applicable to all systems. Some systems, like Precision and Italian Blue Club, just to mention two, are fairly rigid about the actual point count needed to make an active opening statement.

Making an active opening statement is not difficult. You mostly go by what the bidding system says. There is one case, though, that the bidding system does not usually mention, and I would like to review it here.

I call it a *marginal* opening bid. It is a natural opening bid that has one point less than what the bidding system prescribes to make a natural opening bid. Here is my own definition of it. I use it when playing in either SAYC or 2/1GF but not in any other systems I play.

A hand that has one less point than the mandatory opening point count required to make a natural opening statement (13 points in SAYC and 12 points in 2/1GF) may be opened provided it has all of the following:

- one minor of four or more cards
- one major of four cards
- two quick tricks (a quick trick is an ace or a minimum combination king/queen in the same suit)

With such a hand, it is possible to have a rebid and still remain at the level 1 in the auction.

For example, look at the following hand in 2/1GF:

North	
♠	A765
♥	984
♦	KQ72
♣	Q3

Example 10-1

It may be opened with a 1♦ bid.

- If the responder bids 1♥, there is a rebid of 1♠ available.
- If the responder bids 1♠, there is a fit, I can add my one distribution point, making my opening a regular opening count, and I can proceed with going to the next level by bidding 2♠.
- If the partner bids 1NT, implying 6-9 points and less than four diamonds in support, no rebid is needed, and the play will stand in a 1NT contract.
- If the partner bids 2♣, it shows a minimum of 11 points in SAYC or a game force in 2/1GF which, in combination with my 11 points, makes a total of 22 points in SAYC and a very good chance at playing successfully a 2NT contract and game in 2/1GF.
- If the partner bids 2♦, no other bid is necessary if I am not playing inverted minors; otherwise, the game is very likely to be successful in either 3NT or 5♦.
- If the partner bids 2♥ or higher, showing a strong hand in SAYC, almost certainly guarantying the game, and showing a long suit and few points in 2/1GF, I do not need to take any further action.

I encourage you to review the possible responses you would get in both SAYC and 2/1GF if you were to swap the diamonds and the clubs and open 1♣ instead of 1♦.

Do not try this with both majors or with a five-card major, for it does not work.

Opening Statement by the Player in Second Seat

The first bid made by the player in the second seat is an opening statement as well. That statement may be one of the following types, as it is contingent on the type of opening statement the player in first seat (the dealer) made.

- Pass: A **passive opening statement** that shows a hand too weak in points and in shape to start the auction to find a contract after the player in first seat (the dealer) has made a passive opening statement (passed) or the hand is too weak to compete with the other team in the auction where the dealer made an active opening statement (did not pass).

If the dealer passed, the second player may make

- an intermediate opening bid: A **natural active opening statement**. The requirements for such a statement are the same as for the dealer.
- a weak or preemptive opening bid: A **weak active opening statement**. The requirements for such a statement are also the same as for the dealer.
- an artificial bid: An **artificial active opening statement**. The requirements for such a statement are the same as for the dealer as well.

All are similar to the opening statements by the player in first seat.

If the dealer did not pass, the player makes a **reactive opening statement**, and most systems use basically the same point ranges for overcalls, as follows:

Most bidding systems reactive opening statements (opening overcalls)																						
0	1	2	3	4	5	6	7	8	9	10	11	12	13	14	15	16	17	18	19	20	21	22+
Not to overcall with					Weak overcall				Standard overcall									Strong overcall				

Table 10-3

These could be

- a standard opening overcall: A **natural reactive opening statement** that shows a hand with a specific point range and reflects the shape of the hand by naming the long suit, or NT if there is no such long suit, showing the intent to compete in the auction.
- a weak or preemptive opening overcall: A **weak reactive opening statement** that shows a hand with a specific, but weaker, point range and reflects the shape of the hand by naming the long suit, or NT if there is no such long suit, and showing the intent to block the opponents, if not compete in the auction.
- an artificial opening overcall: An **artificial reactive opening statement** that may or may not show a hand with a specific point range and certainly does not reflect the shape of the hand by naming the long suit; it shows the intent to block the opponents, if not compete in the auction.

This list can be charted as below (I do not show the point count again on purpose):

Most bidding systems reactive overcall statements			
Not to overcall with	Weak overcall	Standard overcall	Strong overcall
Passive reactive overcall statement	Weak reactive opening statement	Natural reactive opening statement	Strong reactive opening statement
Table 10-4			

Please check your bidding system for accuracy of the applicable point range.

These are the only active and reactive opening statements that can be made during any auction.

Active and reactive opening bids may themselves have three possible forms:

- Natural active and reactive opening statements come exclusively from the bidding system used and may be converted into a playable contract by the partner, who then simply passes.
- Weak active and reactive opening statements may be originated by either the bidding system used or by conventions agreed upon by the partnership, and they may also be converted into a playable contract by the partner, who then simply passes.
- Artificial active and reactive opening statements are all originated in conventions used by the partnership, with the exception of what is called the strong opening bid (1 ♣ in systems that use 1♣ as the strong bid, 2♣ in those which use it as the strong bid, or some other bid in some other systems), which is a bidding-system conventional bid. These are always forcing statements. In other words, the partner may not simply pass, since no detail about the hand was given in the bid.

There is a fundamental difference between an active opening bid and a reactive opening bid. The difference clearly appears when juxtaposing the active and reactive point range charts.

I will only select one chart here, the 2/1GF one, but the same observation can be easily made regardless of the bidding system used to make that comparison.

The first line will show the active opening statement range; the next line will show the reactive opening statement range.

2/1GF active opening statements																						
0	1	2	3	4	5	6	7	8	9	10	11	12	13	14	15	16	17	18	19	20	21	22+
Not to open with					Weak opening							Natural opening										Strong opening
Not to overcall with					Weak overcall							Natural overcall							Strong overcall			
Table 10-5																						

To illustrate this, let's take an example.

North	East	South	West
Pass	1♠		

Illustration 10-A

North	East	South	West
1♥	1♠		

Illustration 10-B

In both illustrations, East makes the same opening statement of 1♠.

In Illustration 10-A, 1♠ is a natural active opening bid (natural opening bid).

The SAYC system says that in order to make such a bid you need to have 13–21 points and five or more spades, while the 2/1GF System says 12-21 points and five or more spades; the Precision System says 11-15 points and five or more spades; the Italian Blue Club System says 12–16 points and four or more spades; and other systems specify some other range and suit length. Refer to your bidding system book to know what bid applies here.

In Illustration 10-B, 1♠ is a natural reactive opening bid (natural opening overcall). The SAYC system, and many other bidding systems, say that in order to make such a bid, you should have 8-16 points, five or more spades, and two of the three top honors in spades.

Theoretically, that's all you need. In a real game, you will discover very quickly that if you do not have some structure in the hand, something like a singleton or a second four-card suit, the end result may not stand up to your expectations when overcalling with 8 points, especially if you get stuck playing a contract in that suit. If opponents are to play the contract and you are on lead, you would probably be better off not bidding the suit at all, and waiting for the opportunity of the lead to signal your partner you have the suit.

On the other hand, you may have only 8 points and exceptional distribution that may allow you to make a reactive opening statement.

According to the chart of ranges shown above, natural reactive opening belongs to the 8-16 range. The question is now how do you show, in the example above, 13-16 points and five or more spades in one bid when in the second seat?

Well ... You can't. You can only show either thirteen or more points or five or more spades, but not both at the same time. You need at least two bids for that. In other words, if the auction does not come back to you, you will never be able to tell your partner you have an opening hand and five spades.

As a general rule, natural reactive opening statements show, either a long suit, and a wide point range (8 to16) or a narrow point range, but no long suit, as in the example below.

In this auction:

North	East	South	West
1♣	*1NT*		

Example 10-2

1NT is a reactive opening statement (opening overcall by the opener of the other team) to the 1♣ active opening statement made by North (opening bid by the dealer) that shows a point range of 15-18 in SAYC, in other words a four-point spread. It also promises stoppers in clubs but nothing very specific about the other suits except that there is no singleton and no void.

By opposition,

North	East	South	West
1♣	*1♥*		

Example 10-3

1♥ bid is a reactive opening statement to the 1♣ active opening statement made by North that shows a point range of 8-16 in SAYC, in other words, an eight-point spread. It also promises at least five hearts and at least two of the three top honors in that suit, Ace-King, Ace-Queen, or King-Queen (AK, AQ, or KQ) if the hand has less than an opening hand value.

Why is that? One of the reasons is that if E/W ends up playing a contract in hearts, the lack of raw power and lack of trumping power combined would probably result in a failed contract, because the other team's strength would then be overwhelming. E/W would automatically lose two tricks in trump, not to mention that it would not have enough trumping power to compensate. The contract would be unmanageable.

Another reason is that if E/W eventually defends against a N/S contract, laws of probabilities dictate that it is very rare for the defense to be able to cash more than two tricks in any given suit, if that many. Therefore, if the first time the suit is played a trick is not won, the defense will need to establish supremacy in that suit in anticipation of a second round of play in it.

In other words, though it is technically possible that the Queen may make a trick when the King and the Ace are both missing, it requires a very favorable distribution of cards in that suit around the table for it to happen, making the odds fairly poor.

It is therefore a useless and usually a self-destructive reaction to disregard these considerations and make an opening overcall with what some call a *trash suit*.

Opening overcalls are not all natural bids. Some may be artificial, included in the bidding system used or in some convention used on top of the bidding system. They show a hand with a special distribution or a great number of points.

If the artificial bid shows a strong hand, it is not really a problem. The defending side is trying to establish itself as the predominant team and play the contract, just as it would do after making a strong natural bid.

North	East	South	West
1♣	*Dbl*		

Example 10-4

In SAYC, Dbl shows a hand a minimum of 13 and no maximum.

Dbl tends to show a lack of cards in clubs and some length in the other suits, especially in the unbid major suits. I say "tends to" because, with 17 or more points, East may have any shape at all and will be able to define it later, since Dbl is an artificial bid. Therefore, the partner will be forced to ask questions.

If the artificial bid is meant to show a special distribution, it is assuming that the trumping power will compensate for the lack of points during either the play of the hand or the defense against the contract by the opposing team. In that case, the same requirements apply here as for the quality of the suits, but since a second suit is present, there are better chances to find the missing top honors in the partner's hand than in the previous case where the player in second seat made a simple overcall.

When an artificial reactive opening bid is made and the player in third seat passes, the responder in fourth seat may not pass, even with a very bad hand.

We can conclude that to be a valid opening overcall, a reactive opening statement should have a decent point count (many systems recommend 8 or 9 points minimum for natural overcalls and 5 or 6 points minimum for weak and artificial overcalls), one or two suits with length, and two of the three top honors in one of them. Translate that as: The bulk of points should be in the long suits.

I will keep the terminology of passive, active, and reactive opening statements in lieu of Pass, opening bid, and opening overcall along the coming pages because, as we will see in the next sections, the player in third or fourth seat may make an opening bid and an opening overcall too, but these are not statements, and their meaning and usage are different.

Here is the complete list of possible opening statements, for those who like to visualize things. It assumes that the player sitting in North is the dealer.

North	East	South	West
Passive	*Passive*		
Passive	*Active*		
Active	*Passive*		
Active	*Reactive*		

Figure 10-1

Here is the correspondence, to a terminology you already know:

Passive	Pass
Active	Opening bid
Reactive	Opening overcall

Figure 10-2

CHAPTER 11

The Responses to Opening Statements

Opening statements are always followed by a response by the partner, and each team makes at least one response.

North	East	South	West
Opening statement	*Opening statement*	**Response**	Response

Model Extract 11-1

The players in third and fourth seats are always the responders, regardless of what you may have heard through the grapevine, even if the players in first and second seat have passed.

The responder always has more information about the opener's hand than the opener has about the responder's, since the opener always places a bid before the responder does, even if that bid is Pass.

The responder therefore gathers as much information about the opener's hand as possible. The most common way is by asking the opener one or more questions.

The general idea is for the responder to narrow down his/her knowledge of the point range of the opener's hand with the maximum precision possible and to detect a fit of suit between the hands. A *fit* means that both hands combined have a known total of at least eight cards in a suit.

While the responder is doing this, other information may emerge, like the presence of a singleton or a void, or a double fit (when there is a fit in two suits), and that may trigger him/her to reach for new and higher horizons for the contract.

Theoretically, the responder does not have to bid anything that reflects his/her hand's holding, but to be practical, he usually asks questions that imply specific holdings in points and shape. If the opener decides later to override the responder's closing statement, he can do so without putting the team in jeopardy of losing valuable points.

Here is the chart of ranges recommended for SAYC response to natural opening statements. Each range is given a name for ease of recognition:

SAYC active opening statements																						
0	1	2	3	4	5	6	7	8	9	10	11	12	13	14	15	16	17	18	19	20	21	22+
Not to respond with						Standard				Limit			Game forcing									

Chart 11-1

Notice that there is no range mentioned for slam forcing. The responder needs to make at least one game force bid, followed by one or more additional ones, to show slam force values.

This chart is only given as a reference, and its accuracy may be challenged. Different bidding systems may have different range limits, even within themselves. Refer to the system book you are using for better accuracy.

The duties of the responder are, therefore,

- to ask questions forcing answers from the opener;
- to make invitations to the opener; and
- to decide on the level at which a contract will be played.

In the rest of this book, questions will always refer to forcing bids by the captain and invitations to non-forcing questions by the captain.

CHAPTER 12

The Notion of Captainship

At the start of any auction, we just saw that the responder is in the commanding seat. He/she asks the questions and makes the decision of where and how high to play the contract or whether to compete or not with the other team. That's what makes him/her the team captain, at least until he/she releases his/her captainship. We will refer to his/her partner as the crew.

The captain releases his/her captainship when he/she makes a closing statement, converts his/her partner's last answer or opening statement into a contract to play, or makes an invitation.

If the auction continues past that point, the crew becomes the captain, and the process restarts with reversed roles.

In the Components of Conversation chapter, we established four models of auctions, depending on the type of auction ending being used. Model 8-5 shows what happens after the captain makes his/her closing statement and his/her partner does not accept the decision.

North	East	South	West
Opening statement	*Pass*	**Questions**	*Pass*
Answers	*Pass*	**Closing statement**	*Pass*
Questions	*Pass*	Answers	*Pass*
Closing statement	*Pass*	Pass	Pass

Model 8-5

In this case, the captainship shifts from the responder to the opener after the closing statement by the responder.

The new captain remains the captain until he/she, in turn, either passes or makes an invitation or closing statement.

Once both players have dropped captainship, there is no captain in the team any longer, and any bid placed by either player in the team is a standalone bid and is purely competitive.

There is really not a set of rules as to what the captain should do next or how many questions he/she is supposed to ask. That determination is really left to the captain, who can act in one of four possible ways, by:

- passing;
- asking a question;
- making an invitation; or
- making a closing statement.

And that is what our next chapters are about.

Gerard's Tidbit of the Night: Dummy Claim

When you are the dummy, even if you know that the declarer can claim the rest of the tricks, do not sing to him/her the song "Oh My Darling Claiming Time." The director may be summoned, and he will not call you darling!

CHAPTER 13

Pass by the Captain

If the other team has already withdrawn from the auction, a pass by the captain is the conversion of the last bid by the crew into a contract to play. However, if the other team has not withdrawn from the auction, then Pass is a request to withdraw from it.

In either case, the captain makes a decision, and the crew is advised to respect that decision, unless he/she has not disclosed his/her hand totally, either in points or in shape.

By passing, the captain also gives up his/her captainship. If the auction is relaunched by the crew, the crew will then become the new captain for the team, and the ex-captain will be demoted to the rank of crew.

The captain may pass at any time during an auction, including in the first round of auction, unless the opening statement is artificial. In this case, he must ask for details about the crew's hand before taking the proper decision step.

In the auction as in SAYC, where the opening statement is artificial:

North	East	South	West
2♣	*Pass*	Bid?	

Example 13-1

South may not pass, even though he is the captain at that stage of the bidding, because 2♣ is an artificial bid that needs some explanations. In this specific case, 2♣ showing a game force hand in SAYC forces the captain to ask questions until he/she has a good idea of the crew's holding in points and distribution of suits. Usually game level will be reached.

In an auction as in SAYC, where the opening statement is natural:

North	East	South	West
1♣	*Pass*	**Bid?**	

Example 13-2

Even though 1♣ only promises a three-card club suit, South, as captain, may pass if his/her holding is very weak.

In an auction as in SAYC, where the opening is weak and natural:

North	East	South	West
3♣	*Pass*	**Bid?**	

Example 13-3

It is left to the discretion of the captain whether to go on or not. His/her decision will, of course, be guided by his/her knowledge that the crew has a preemptive hand (check your bidding system book for the requirements for such a bid) and the content of his/her own hand.

Even in an auction that has gone beyond the first round of bidding, the same principle applies. In the example below, we will assume that North has a hand stronger than a regular opening call, let's say 17-21 points, and will show that by making what is called a reverse bid, as in SAYC:

North	East	South	West
1♣	*Pass*	1♠	*Pass*
2♥	*Pass*	**Bid?**	

Example 13-4

South, as the team's captain, is entitled to pass such a bid.

Let's not debate here the merits or lack thereof in passing such an auction. Even if it is not always a wise decision, it still is an option that is available to South, as responder and captain of the N/S team.

The above were all cases in which the N/S team went on the offensive, but when the E/W is competing, the captain of the E/W team also makes the decisions for that team.

Here is a typical example of an occasion when the E/W team has to decide whether competing is warranted or not with the following auction:

North	East	South	West
1♣	*1♠*	**1NT**	Pass

Example 13-5

South is the current captain for the N/S team, and West is the current captain for the E/W team.

Pass by West (captain of the E/W team) is a closing statement advising East (the crew of the E/W team) not to compete any further in the auction. West's decision is based on his/her knowledge that East has a minimum of 8 points or whatever number of points the E/W team is using as minimum for overcalls.

In all cases, one thing is constant: As we already mentioned earlier in this chapter, a pass by the captain of the E/W team, since it is a passive response, will also mark the end of his/her captainship.

In other words, if the crew bids anything, the crew will become the new captain and collect all the privileges and duties of the captainship.

If East, in our example, makes a new bid, he/she will take over the captainship.

We will review the nature of the bids made by the captain of the competing team in a later chapter.

CHAPTER 14

Invitations by the Captain

There are two specific situations in which the captain may make an invitation:

- in the first round of auction
- later on in the auction

Invitation During the First Round of Auctions

In case players in first and second seats have passed, no opening bid has been made yet. Therefore logic commands that if an opening bid is ever to be placed, it will have to be by either the player in third or fourth seat.

To help visualize:

North	East	South	West
Opening statement	*Opening statement*	**Response**	*Response*
Pass	*Pass*	**Opening bid**	

Illustration 14-A

Or

North	East	South	West
Opening statement	*Opening statement*	**Response**	*Response*
Pass	*Pass*	Pass	***Opening bid***

Illustration 14-B

What is the difference between an opening bid by the player in first or second seat and an opening bid by the player in third or fourth seat?

The opening bid by the player in first or second seat is an opening statement, while the opening bid by the player in third or fourth seat is an invitation.

For ease of comprehension, in this upcoming section I will use the term *responder*, but make no mistake, the responder is the current captain of the team, in charge, with all the duties and having all the rights attached to the notion of captainship.

In the auction, in the SAYC system:

North	East	South	West
Pass	*Pass*	**1♥**	

Example 14-1

1♥ is a natural opening bid to perform as an invitation. North's opening statement is Pass, showing a hand below opening standards, and South is aware of it when his/her turn to bid comes up. The invitation by South then is "Hey, partner! If your hand is not the pits, tell me if we can play something better than a 1 ♥ contract!" and in some systems, as in SAYC and 2/1GF, the constraints for such a bid are not as stringent as for an opening bid made as an opening statement. South does not need to have a full opening hand point count and/or may have four hearts only, in opposition to a 1♥ opening statement, which shows a 13-21 point range and a hand with five or more hearts.

When the opening bid is an active opening statement (in first or second seat), there has not been any prior bid for that side. Therefore, there is no presumption about the partner's holding in points nor in shape, and the meaning of opening statements is set according to the bidding system used. As for the contract to be reached, the sky is the limit.

By opposition, when the opening bid is an invitation (third or fourth seat), the responder already knows that his/her partner has a bad hand and already knows there are limitations on how far the auction can go. Bidding a slam is very unlikely, if not impossible, without a special distribution or exceptional strength in the responder's hand.

Even though bidding systems recommend specific parameters in points and shape for an opening bid in third and fourth seats, they leave more leeway for the actual point count and shape. Your convention card actually has an area reserved for you to fill with the parameters you will be using to make opening bids in third and fourth seat.

Weak opening bids by the responder work the same as natural opening bids.

Artificial opening bids follow the same principle. When made by the opener, they are opening statements, but when made by the responder, they should be invitations. Being artificial, in either case they actually are forcing for a rebid.

In the auction below, in the SAYC system,

North	East	South	West
Pass	*Pass*	2♣	

Example 14-2

North has already passed, showing a poor hand unworthy of any opening bid, regular or even weak.

The 2♣ by South is a question to North that means "How bad is your hand?" It implies that South's hand is very powerful or has a very unbalanced structure, and it shows a strong intent to reach game, provided that the opening statement bidder has enough to help (but not forcibly the 22 or more points or eight and a half tricks that the same bid means as an opening statement).

The same thing happens if the player in fourth seat makes the opening bid using a natural bid, as in:

North	East	South	West
Pass	*Pass*	**Pass**	*1♥*

Example 14-3

Or an artificial bid, like:

North	East	South	West
Pass	*Pass*	Pass	*2♣*

Example 14-4

What was true for an opening bid in third seat is also true for an opening bid in fourth seat.

Natural and weak opening bids by the responder are invitational. The opener, having made a passive opening statement, may have no values at all in his/her hand and may accept or refuse the invitation by the responder.

Artificial opening bids by the responder force a rebid by the partner, as does any artificial bid.

The same concept applies to opening overcalls by the responder.

In this auction, in the SAYC system,

North	East	South	West
Pass	*1♣*	1♥	

Example 14-5

1♥ is a question. North's opening statement was Pass, showing a hand below opening standards, and South is aware of it when his/her turn to bid comes up. The question by South then is "Hey, partner! Is your hand that bad that you can't compete at all in the auction?"

The player who made a passive opening statement may refuse the invitation to compete.

From this, we can conclude that opening bids and opening overcalls by the responder are only invitational, unless they are artificial.

The last case of invitational bids is the one of *balancing bids*.

The definition of a balancing bid is one that follows two successive passes after the dealer has made an active opening statement, as in this example:

North	East	South	West
1♣	*Pass*	Pass	**Bid?**

Example 14-6

During the first round of auctions, most natural balancing bids have the same meaning as bids placed in the second seat. Nevertheless, two of them are notoriously different: 1NT and Dbl.

The well-known balancing 1NT usually shows a lesser value in points than the same bid placed in second seat, 11-14 points in SAYC and 2/1GF, and implies a balanced hand having some cards in the opponent's suit. Refer to your bidding system to know the accurate point range in that system.

The other one is Dbl, an artificial bid, which I call an SOS double, even though it is traditionally called a balancing double. It does not necessarily imply an opening hand, as it does in second seat, but a balanced hand that implies the absence of cards in the opponent's suit and is requesting the partner to bid something—anything.

Invitation During the Next Rounds of Auctions

The other case may happen during the course of the auctions. To make it simple and clear, let's choose an auction, as in SAYC:

North	East	South	West
1♣	*Pass*	1♥	*Pass*
2♥	*Pass*	3♥	

Example 14-7

The 2♥ answer by North shows a fit in hearts, assuming that the captain's 1♥ question implies the presence of a minimum of four hearts in his/her hand.

The rebid of 3♥ by the captain, after the fit has been established in hearts, is meant to ask North to bid 4♥ with the maximum point count in his/her hand or to pass with less than the maximum.

We can define this type of invitation as a raise of the last bid by the crew below game level or slam level, depending on the level reached in the auction.

In Example 14-7, game level was not reached; therefore, the invitation is to play at the 4♥ game level.

This is equally true when the auction reaches a game level.

In the auction, in SAYC,

North	East	South	West
1♣	*Pass*	1♥	*Pass*
4♥	*Pass*	5♥	

Example 14-8

The 5♥ is an invitation to play at the level of 6♥.

Let's go one step further by declaring that in the auction, in SAYC,

North	East	South	West
1♣	*Pass*	1♥	*Pass*
3NT	*Pass*	4NT	

Example 14-9

The 4NT is an invitation to play in 6NT and never the start of the Blackwood convention, nor of the Roman Key Card convention.

There is one more case that we need to consider, which is an extension of Example 14-9. In the auction, also in SAYC,

North	East	South	West
1♣	*Pass*	1♥	*Pass*
3NT	*Pass*	5NT	

Example 14-10

The 5NT is an invitation to play in 7NT, not in 6NT. If North does not have enough values to bid 7NT, bidding 6NT is a refusal, but passing 5NT is not a valid option.

It is easy to understand that if the captain had bid 6NT, it could not possibly have been an invitation to 7NT, since 6NT is not an intermediary level. Therefore, the only intermediary level to make an invitation to 7NT is, indeed, 5NT.

I personally do not care too much for invitational raises, because they force the crew to make a decision without really knowing with certainty the content of the captain's hand.

Nevertheless, invitational raises exist and cannot be simply ignored.

We will find in a later chapter another way, much more elegant and more modern, to make such an invitation.

CHAPTER 15

Answers to Captain's Invitations

Before getting involved with the meaning of the various positive answers, let's repeat here that invitations in bridge may be passed. In other words, the crew may always pass any invitation if he/she deems his/her hand not good enough to accept it.

Now there remains the case when an invitation is accepted. There is a difference in the way the crew answers to an invitation, depending on when the invitation takes place.

To an opening bid made by the captain (the responder), the crew (the passed hand) may choose to

- support the named suit;
- show his/her dislike for the named suit by showing a preferential suit (usually his/her longest);
- show his/her dislike for the named suit by bidding NT (usually because the potential preferential suit has already been bid by the opponents); or
- pass.

As example, in an auction starting like, in SAYC:

North	East	South	West
Pass	*Pass*	1♠	*Pass*
Bid?			

Example 15-1

Notice that the rebid is a bid by a passed hand.

With support in the suit, the responses may be, in function of the point count of the hand:

SAYC responses to opening bid by responder																						
0	1	2	3	4	5	6	7	8	9	10	11	12	13	14	15	16	17	18	19	20	21	22+
Not to respond with						Standard				Limit												
Pass						2♠				3♠			Show of splinter with a limit hand is equivalent to a game force in the suit.									

Chart 15-1

With no support in the suit and a preferential diamond suit (four or more diamonds), the responses may be, in function of the point count of the hand:

SAYC responses to opening bid by responder																						
0	1	2	3	4	5	6	7	8	9	10	11	12	13	14	15	16	17	18	19	20	21	22+
Not to respond with						Standard				Limit			Game force									
Pass						2♦				3♦												

Chart 15-2

With no support in the suit and no biddable preferential, the responses may be, in function of the point count of the hand:

SAYC responses to opening bid by responder			
0 1 2 3 4 5	6 7 8 9	10 11 12	13 14 15 16 17 18 19 20 21 22+
Not to respond with	Standard	Limit	Game force
Pass	1NT	2NT	

Chart 15-3

This covers the case of the responder making an opening bid after the dealer has passed.

To any other invitation made by the captain, acceptance or refusal of the invitation is exclusively a question of points within the range advertised in the opening statement, and the invitation is always in the last called suit. The captain's partner accepts the invitation with the top of the range or refuses it with less than the top.

In an auction like this one,

North	East	South	West
1♥	*Pass*	2♥	*Pass*
Bid?			

Example 15-2

the possible rebids by North are, in function of the point count:

2/1GF active opening statements																					
0	1	2	3	4	5	6	7	8	9	10	11	12	13	14	15	16	17	18	19	20	21 22+
													Pass			3♥ or game try bid			4♥		

Chart 15-4

The game try bid by North, usually a minor suit bid at the 3 level, is meant to ask South's assistance to make the final determination whether to bid game or not.

Any acceptance to an invitation that is not a raise of one of the captain's named suits is denying support for these suits, for instance,

North	East	South	West
1♥	*Pass*	1♠	*Pass*
2♦	*Pass*	2♠	*Pass*
2NT			

Example 15-3

denies having two spades.

Note that this bid is very seldom used, because it does not promise a club suit. South may not have any other available offer to make and simply converts 2NT into the final contract, which may be lethal to the team.

On the principle that only the captain may make an invitation, ask questions, and make decisions, the crew bids are never forcing.

In case the captain's partner cannot support the captain's suit and does not (or is not willing to) show a preferential suit, he/she may bid NT as an acceptance to an invitation.

The NT bid, used as acceptance to an invitation made by the captain, is a negative answer and does not necessarily reflect the possession of a balanced hand or a stopper in all the unbid suits named by the team.

Pass by the captain transforms that answer into a contract to play.

Gerard's Tip of the Night: Declarer's Play

Each declarer's play is like a battle. Prepare for battle. Count your winning tricks if the contract plays in NT, your losing tricks if the contract plays in a suit. Make a plan of attack to better your chances of changing losing tricks into winning ones.

CHAPTER 16

Questions by the Captain

Questions, as we defined them earlier, are bids placed by the captain that inquire about the partner's hand. The partner must provide an answer other than Pass. It is as if you ask the time of somebody—you expect an answer.

The principle remains the same for the offense and competing teams alike.

One question may not be enough to uncover the full value of the partner's hand. More questions may follow, each one deserving its own answer.

The auction model then looks like this:

North	East	South	West
Opening statement	*Opening statement*	**Question 1**	*Question 1*
Answer 1	*Answer 1*	**Question 2**	*Question 2*
Answer 2	*Answer 2*	**Question 3**	*Question 3*
Answer 3	*Answer 3*	**Etc.**	Etc.

Model Extract 16-1

Questions 1, 2, 3, etc. are all questions asked in response to the opening statement, and the player who makes these responses is called the responder.

There are two types of questions:

- natural
- artificial

Natural means that the bid is natural. In other words, the captain is implying he has some length in the suit he/she bids.

In any of these auctions, in SAYC or 2/1GF, where South is the captain:

North	East	South	West
1♣	*Pass*	1♥	

Example 16-1

North	East	South	West
Pass	*Pass*	1♣	*Pass*
1♦	*Pass*	1♥	

Example 16-2

North	East	South	West
Pass	*Pass*	1♣	*Pass*
1♦	*Pass*	2♥	

Example 16-3

North	East	South	West
Pass	*Pass*	1♣	*Pass*
1♠	*Pass*	2♥	

Example 16-4

1♥ and 2♥ are questions. 1♥ does not imply any particular strength, but 2♥ implies a hand with opening hand strength.

In some systems, though, like 2/1GF, a new suit named using a jump is not a question but a closing statement, as we will see later on.

In the SAYC system, a jump is also a question. For instance:

North	East	South	West
1♣	*Pass*	2♥	

Example 16-5

Where 2♥ implies a hand that has a minimum value of an opening hand. But this is *not* the case in 2/1GF, where such a bid implies a weak hand.

Artificial means that the captain's bid does not imply anything concerning the shape or strength of his/her hand.

SAYC is not very rich in artificial bids, so let's retreat toward systems that have more of them.

In the auction in 2/1GF,

North	East	South	West
1♠	*Pass*	1NT	

Example 16-6

1NT is an artificial bid that does not imply a balanced hand of any sort but is asking North to give more details about his/her hand. North, therefore, may not pass, regardless of his/her holding.

Any bid naming a new suit by the captain, after an active opening bid or a reactive opening overcall has been made, that does not imply a weak hand, is a question that must be answered.

Relays are artificial bids that a player makes after his/her partner has made an artificial call and the opponent in between has passed. They are used to allow the maker of the artificial call to rebid.

An example of a relay in the SAYC system would be:

North	East	South	West
2♣	*Pass*	2♦	

Example 16-7

Here, 2♦ simply waits for North to make a rebid that will give some idea about the shape of his/her hand. That bid is traditionally called a waiting bid and does not mean the hand is worth nothing.

There are two levels of force in a question:

- one-round force
- game force

Here is an example in which we can easily see the difference between the SAYC and the 2/1GF systems:

North	East	South	West
1♥	*Pass*	**2♣**	

Example 16-8

Alternately:

North	East	South	West
Pass	*1♥*	**Pass**	2♣

Example 16-9

The 2♣ response is forcing, because it is a new suit, but it is only forcing for one round in SAYC, while it is forcing to game in the 2/1GF system.

In both cases, 2♣ may not be passed by North, but in SAYC, for instance, unless South keeps making forcing bids, North does not have to bid after his/her reply to the 2♣.

In the 2/1GF system, 2♣ is forcing to game, meaning that South does not have to ask any more questions after his/her original one, because North is not allowed to pass until game has been reached. Just en passant, if South does not like what he/she hears as response, he/she is allowed to change his/her mind and abort the auction before reaching game. But only South can do that.

A game-force bid is not necessary to reach game. It can be replaced by a cascade of one round forcing bids, at the expense of purity of the auction.

Look at this auction, in 2/1GF:

North	East	South	West
1♥	*Pass*	1NT	*Pass*
2♦	*Pass*	2♠	*Pass*
2NT	*Pass*	3♣	*Pass*
3NT	*Pass*	**Pass**	Pass

Example 16-10

All three bids by South are forcing. 1NT is forcing one round as an artificial bid. The 2♠ and 3♣ are forcing, because they are new suits. The end result is that N/S team reached 3NT, even though the route chosen is rather unorthodox.

A shortcut for this auction would be:

North	East	South	West
1♥	*Pass*	2♣	*Pass*
2♦	*Pass*	3NT	*Pass*
Pass	*Pass*		

Example 16-11

It is a much shorter auction landing in the same contract, and only one question is asked: 2♣.

The first part of the chapter was dedicated to questions asked of the maker of an active opening statement.

The next part is reserved for questions asked of the maker of a reactive opening statement.

As we saw in a previous chapter, a reactive opening statement (overcall) is the first bid made by the player in second seat, provided that the dealer made an active opening bid (opening bid).

To make this statement more understandable, using our model, it would be represented as:

North	East	South	West
Opening statement	*Opening statement*	Response	*Response*
Active	*Reactive*	Any bid	***This bid!***
Opening bid	*Opening overcall*		

Model Extract 16-2

If you still have a hard time visualizing it, let's take an example:

North	East	South	West
1♥	*1♠*	Pass	Bid?

Example 16-12

The player in fourth seat is the most informed player of all the players around the table. He has knowledge of what the other players may or may not have in their hands.

Armed with this knowledge, his/her task is to decide whether or not he will force, encourage, or discourage his/her side to compete with the dealer's side.

This is also probably the most difficult situation to be in during any auction in bridge. The player in fourth seat has to use his/her best judgment when making the decision.

The question is: Can he/she delay his/her choice of deciding to compete with the dealer's team or not?

If the reactive opening statement is a strong bid or an artificial bid, the response to that question is usually no. He/she then asks his/her partner to further describe his/her hand, using a natural or an artificial bid. The type of bid does not actually matter that much, but preference will be given to a useful bid rather than a neutral bid.

North	East	South	West
1♦	1♠	1NT	Dbl

Example 16-13

In the SAYC system, Dbl in the fourth seat is not a very helpful bid. It shows some points value, but no clear question is actually asked, and East will probably be in a difficult spot when his/her turn to rebid comes. The only thing that East knows is that his/her partner has decided to compete ... but how? Will he/she compete in spades, in NT, or in some other suit?

Good players always try to avoid putting their partners in a tough situation.

Of course, the problem does not occur if support doubles are used. Dbl then implies three-card support and is asking East to continue competing with a decent hand.

CHAPTER 17

Answers to Captain's Questions

Answers to the captain's questions are always natural, unless they are part of a convention and the convention calls for artificial answers.

We will not deal with conventions at this point, since there is a chapter dedicated to this specific subject.

In case you are confused, I remind you that in the auction in 2/1GF,

North	East	South	West
1♥	1♠	2♥	Pass
3♣	Pass		

Example 17 1

The 2♥ by the responder (and captain) is not a forcing bid. It is a closing statement that shows a fit in hearts and not enough values to reach game on his/her own decision.

The opener chooses to override the closing statement by South and becomes the new captain of the team.

In this specific example, the 3♣ bid by the new captain is asking South to answer by either bidding 3♥ to show a weak hand, or anything else (except Pass) to show top of the range for a 2♥ bid.

This bid is called a *game try* and does not imply possession of any clubs at all. It is an artificial bid.

The answer to a question by the captain shows

- variable levels in strength:

  o lower part of the range; or

  o upper part of the range;

- and by priority:

  o support for the captain's named suit, if any (by bidding the captain's suit);

  o a side suit, if such a suit exists, in case of lack of support in captain's named suit (by bidding that side suit);

  o more than the number of cards required by the system in the original suit bid (by repeating the original suit); and, finally,

  o denial of all of the above (by bidding NT).

Pass is never a valid answer to any of the captain's questions.

It is a mistake to believe that the answer of NT to a captain's question means that all the missing suits have a stopper or even that the hand contains cards in all suits. NT is only a denial answer, nothing more.

In this auction, in SAYC,

North	East	South	West
1♥	*Pass*	1♠	*Pass*
1NT			

Example 17-2

1NT does not promise any holding in clubs or diamonds. North's hand may very well look like this:

North	
♠	KJ5
♥	K9764
♦	AQ5
♣	J2

Example 17-2A

He/she may still bid 1NT, denying a fit in spades, having a second biddable suit or the mandatory six hearts to rebid hearts.

Only the captain may convert a NT bid by his/her partner into a contract to play.

CHAPTER 18

Closing Statements by Captain

There always comes a point when the captain has to put an end to questions and must make a decision as to what contract should be played. He has to pick the trump suit (or NT if no suit fit was found), as well as its level, whether part score, game, small slam, or grand slam.

We saw earlier that he can simply pass and convert the last bid by his/her partner into a contract to play if the other team has withdrawn from the auction, or pass and withdraw from the auction if the other team is still active in the auction.

We also saw that the captain may make an invitation to play a suit or a NT contract in game, small-slam, or grand-slam level.

The captain may also make a closing statement, which is, in fact, a proposal of contract to play.

To do that, he must choose one of the suits already bid by the team, or NT, if he/she could not establish an eight-card fit.

Again, a new suit cannot be a closing statement. It always is a question.

Now comes the decision as to what level to select. Is the contract being played as a *partial* game, small slam, or grand slam?

It all depends on the combined point value between the crew's hand and the captain's.

During the course of the auction, the captain should have obtained from the partner a fairly narrow evaluation of his/her point range. By adding his/her own HCPs and distribution points, he/she then has a specific global point range and should be able to determine at what level to play the contract.

According to Charles Henry Goren, one of the highest authorities of all time on the game, when combining the point values in both partners hand together, an average player needs 25 points to play a 3NT contract, 27 to play a contract in four of a major, 29 points to play a contract in five of a minor, 33 in a small slam, and 37 in a grand slam.

A new breed of highly gifted players is actually able to successfully play 3NT with 24 points, four in a major with 25 points, five in a minor with 27 points, a small slam with 30 points, and a grand slam with 34 points.

The bottom line is that, depending on how good you are with declarer's play, you can select one of these scales and, as captain, set the contract level according to that, if you will be playing it. You need to figure out how good your partner is and decide which scale to use, if he/she is to play it. The scale might be different. But please, please—be diplomatic about it! Don't tell your partner you decided to stay in a partial contract because you did not think he could make a 3NT contract with only 24 points.

All jokes aside, look at the following auction, in SAYC:

North	East	South	West
1♥	*Pass*	1♠	*Pass*
2♣	*Pass*	2♥	

Example 18-1

North	East	South	West
1♥	*Pass*	1♠	*Pass*
2♣	*Pass*	2♠	

Example 18-2

North	East	South	West
1♥	*Pass*	1♠	*Pass*
2♣	*Pass*	2NT	

Example 18-3

The last bid by South, the captain of the N/S team, is the proposal to play in the named contract at the mentioned level.

In the first case, the captain declares a fit with the crew's hand; in the second case, a longer suit than usual; and in the third case; a lack of fit.

The crew will accept to play any of these contracts, unless he/she made a bidding error to start with. An example of a bidding error would be North rebidding 2♣ with 17 or more points. But I know you don't do that—I have never done that in my entire life!

To make sure that we are on the same wavelength, before closing this chapter, I feel that it is necessary to compare two auctions that seem similar but are not at all.

Using the first of the auctions above,

North	East	South	West
1♥	*Pass*	1♠	*Pass*
2♣	*Pass*	2♥	

Example 18-1

let's compare it to:

North	East	South	West
		Pass	*Pass*
1♥	*Pass*	1♠	*Pass*
2♣	*Pass*	2♥	

Example 18-4

Both auctions look similar, but in the second case, two passes are made before the opening bid of 1♥.

In the first case, North makes an active opening statement, and South is the captain.

In the second case, South makes a passive opening statement, and North is the captain.

In the first case, 2♥ is a closing statement by the captain, which normally marks the end of the auction.

In the second case, 2♥ is the answer to the 2♣ question asked by the captain in North. A 2♥ may show two or three hearts in support, but it denies support of clubs. It also denies diamonds, since the natural answer with a diamond suit would be 2NT.

By deduction, we can say that South has three hearts, at most; three diamonds, at most; and three clubs, at most.

Having selected not to support hearts with three cards, South's holding in spades has to be strong enough to justify that decision with a minimum hand, which we already know South has.

North's choices are, therefore, to either take the risk of playing in 2♥ with a probable seven-card fit by passing, ask 3♦ as a new question, and wait for the answer before making a determination of where to play the contract with less than three spades, support spades with three pieces, and bid 3♠; or to declare a no fit and bid 2NT.

I wish to underline here that more important than the examples themselves is the difference that exists between making the same bid as captain or as partner of the captain.

Gerard's Tip of the Night: Play Like the Experts

When making an opening lead against a slam lead, by preference, King from King-Queen, or your Ace, or a high card in a bad suit—unless there's a compelling reason not to.

CHAPTER 19

Integration of Artificial Bids in Auctions

We have established that artificial bids can be and are used in opening statements and during the course of auctions.

We have also established that, when only one team participates in an auction, only the captain may make such artificial bids. The crew may only use natural bids, unless the artificial bid by the captain calls for an artificial answer. This does happen when the captain asks for a relay, for instance, and that's the sign that the artificial bid by the captain is actually the first step in a complex convention.

There is one case missing. It is the case of artificial bids placed by the crew as an answer to the captain, when the opponents have entered the auction, and the crew uses the opponent's bid as a platform for the answer to the captain's question.

An example of this would be, in 2/1GF:

North	East	South	West
1♥	1♠	2♣	*Pass*
2♠			

Example 19-1

In this auction, 2♠ is an artificial answer to the 2♣ question asked by the captain of the N/S team. It is artificial because it does not mean the possession of spades in the hand. The opponent has already declared having spades. It is, rather, a strong bid that shows an above-average strength in points and support for clubs.

Because 2♠ is artificial, it is logical to believe that it also is a forcing bid, encouraging the captain to reach, at least, game.

Why not use a natural answer instead of an artificial bid?

Let's suppose that North makes a natural answer to the 2♣ question, showing a stronger hand than average and support for clubs.

That auction now looks like this:

North	East	South	West
1♥	1♠	2♣	*Pass*
4♣			

Example 19-2

Both auctions show the same hand in North.

The difference is that, with answering 4♣, it is not possible anymore to play a 3NT contract, 4♣ being higher than 3NT. In order to reach game, South would have to bid 5♣, requiring more tricks and yielding fewer scoring points than 3NT, in case some overtricks can be made.

In modern bidding techniques, 4♣ as an answer shows a definite interest for slam in clubs, when 2♠ would let the captain decide where to place the contract.

In essence, even the answer of 4♣ is not totally natural anymore, but artificial, showing a higher-than-standard number of points and support in clubs and suggesting the captain think about slam. The "suggesting" part is what makes it artificial.

We defined artificial bids as not necessarily reflecting the content of a hand. Again, an opening bid of 2♣ does not mean that the hand has any clubs at all. Artificial bids are meant to tell the partner that the hand has either a very unusual distribution, or a very unusual point count—or both.

All conventions have the same purpose: to help find a suit fit if any can be found and to delimit, with as much precision as possible, the point count in the combination of both partners' hands.

Technically, a convention that consists of a single bid replaces a natural bid in the bidding system used. A convention that uses more than one bid is triggered by one artificial bid that replaces a natural bid of the bidding system used.

Dbl and RDbl do not modify the level of the auctions, but they may be either natural or artificial bids. In the old days of bridge, Dbl used to mean "Opponents, you are not going to make that contract!" and RDbl by the opponents meant "Watch me!" In modern bridge, the concept of penalty Dbl still exists but is limited to bids higher than a specified level, either by the bidding system used or by partnership agreement.

All doubles and redoubles below game level, by default—or at or below a specified level, by partnership agreement—have an artificial meaning, and as any artificial bid, they require a new bid by the partner.

They are Takeout Dbl and Takeout RDbl, with different reasons for the takeout. They mostly are negative, positive, support, or balancing, but they can also sometimes be simple takeout.

A negative Dbl originally shows the unbid suits normally, by four cards. In auctions such as this one,

North	East	South	West
1♣	*1♥*	Dbl	

Example 19-3

Dbl is used to show a hand containing four spades and four diamonds and undefined point count.

The original treatment of negative double has greatly evolved in recent years. Today, such a bid implies four cards in the unbid major and about any holding in the unbid minor when the double is done by the captain, but shows both missing suits by four when the double is done by the crew.

North	East	South	West
		Pass	*Pass*
1♣	*1♥*	Dbl	

Example 19-4

The double here shows four spades and four diamonds.

If both named suits are major suits, as in this example,

North	East	South	West
1♠	*2♥*	Dbl	

Example 19-5

or minor suits, like this one,

North	East	South	West
1♣	*1♦*	Dbl	

Example 19-6

it also always implies four cards in the unbid suits, therefore, four clubs and four diamonds in the first case, and four hearts and four spades in the second case.

Some players seem to think that making a negative double with a five-card major is right. It is not, regardless of the cards held in that suit.

Experience proves the theory to be true: a trump suit that does not contain any honor may still yield a contract at game level. The lack of quality in the trump suit is compensated for by the outstanding quality of the rest of the hand, else the contract could not have been bid altogether.

A negative Dbl is primarily meant to find a four-four fit in a major, a fit that would have been impossible to find any other way, especially when playing a five-card bidding system, where opening a four-card suit is most unwelcome. By extension, when a major fit cannot be found, establishing a four-four fit in a minor might be useful, but most of the time, NT is a much better spot in which to land.

Responsive doubles are another kind of double, but they also show four-card support. Here is an example of one:

North	East	South	West
1♥	*Dbl*	2♦	*Dbl*

Example 19-7

If the dealer shows 1♥ now, it is a natural active opening statement showing a certain number of hearts (four or more in a four-card bidding systems and five or more in a five-card system) and an opening hand.

Dbl by East is for takeout; it is a reactive opening statement that shows at least an opening hand. If just used as an opening hand, it also promises four spades, but with 17 points or more, it does not promise any particular distribution. Remember this point during the rest of this example study.

A 2♦ is a question by the captain of the N/S team, and it implies some points value; otherwise, asking a question would have been out of line.

The captain of the E/W team, sitting West, also has a few points and four spades in hand.

Let's calculate each hand value:

North has 12+ points
East has 12+ points
South has 6+ points
West has 6+ points

If each player has the minimum, we get a total of 36 points, 4 points short of the 40 points that a bridge deck of cards is supposed to contain. If this is not the case, you might want to play bridge with other people!

Let's attribute the missing 4 points to East. East would have a maximum possible of 16 points, 1 point short of what East would need to overcall with a double showing 17+ points and any shape of hand. East has to have four spades in hand.

Does West have to Dbl, too, in order to show four spades? The answer is no, but since they have a small number of points, isn't it natural that if a contract in hearts were to be played by the

E/W side, then East, who has the greatest number of points in the team, would play it?

This is exactly why this artificial bid, the responsive Dbl, was invented.

There is another type of artificial double used in modern bridge that is worth reviewing here, because it will probably eventually be incorporated into all bidding systems. It is the support double and its extension, the support redouble.

A typical use of support double shows in this auction

North	East	South	West
1♥	1♠	2♣	Dbl

Example 19-8

and support redouble in this auction:

North	East	South	West
1♥	1♠	Dbl	RDbl

Example 19-9

Both Dbl and RDbl by West here show exactly three-card support to the five spades promised by East.

In the old days, again, West used to bid 2♠, instead of doubling, but this has two major inconveniences. 1) The 1♠ reactive opening bid by East did not promise an opening hand but merely a minimum of around 9 points and five spades. The 2♠ did not imply having any specific number of spades other than a minimum of three, forcing East to guess what to do next. 2) More importantly, the auction was pushed to the level of two, and playing at such a level is a difficult thing to do without fairly good hands either in points or distribution. This type of auction, because of its imprecision, left the E/W team in the dark as far as how good the chances of making the contract were if the N/S team withdrew prematurely from the auction.

For teams using negative, responsive, and support doubles, some of the guessing game disappears. In an auctions like this one,

North	East	South	West
Pass	*1♠*	**2♣**	Dbl

Example 19-10

where West uses a negative double, as well as this one,

North	East	South	West
1♥	*Dbl*	**2♣**	Dbl

Example 19-11

where West uses a responsive double, and

North	East	South	West
1♥	*1♠*	**2♣**	**2♠**

Example 19-12

this one, where West uses a natural support bid, West implies having four spades in support, while in this one,

North	East	South	West
1♥	*1♠*	**2♣**	Dbl

Example 19-13

where West uses a support double, and

North	East	South	West
1♥	*1♠*	**Dbl**	RDbl

Example 19-14

where West uses a support redouble after South uses a negative double, West implies having only three spades in support.

Balancing doubles and outright takeout doubles are also artificial doubles, but much more imprecise. They are just a way for a player to ask his/her partner to rebid again without implying any specific reason.

Other artificial bids and conventions exist—many of them. My intention, again, is not to make a list and explain each one of them but to review the tools that are being used when conversing in the bridge language

Now that you have acquired the panoply of the perfect bridge player, let's review in a more global way the strategies you may use to reach your contracts or force the opponents to miss theirs.

CHAPTER 20

Bidding Contracts Without Interference

Sometimes, it is obvious which is the offensive team. If an auction, in any system, starts this way,

North	East	South	West
1♣	*Pass*	1♠	Pass

Auction 20-1

N/S has established its offensive dominance, regardless of the meaning of the 1♣ and 1♠ bids. E/W will probably not compete for the contract on this hand, and for the rest of this auction, N/S will play the questions/answers game, probably without interference.

The 1♣ bid in the SAYC system shows a minimum of 13 points and a maximum limit of 21 points. If North had 22 or more points, he/she would have been well advised to open with 2♣.

The 1♠ question implies a minimum of 6 points and a maximum of 27 points (the 40 points contained in the deck, minus the minimum number of points held in North's hand).

Seen from the point of view of South, the combination between both hands shows:

- a minimum of its hand's points plus 13 points; and
- a maximum of its hand's points plus 21 points.

From North point of view, even though the South bid only implies a minimum of 6 points, the team probably has a minimum of its hand's points plus 6 points and a maximum of 40 minus his/her own hand's points. Remember, though, that it does not really matter what North thinks at that point. South will be asking the questions and making an assessment of the best contract in which to play.

For the other team, altogether, the minimum potential point spread is 19-40, minus whatever each opponent actually counts in his/her own hand.

I'll let you figure the mathematics of it.

By asking the relevant questions, South should be able to narrow down that spread within 4 points in the next round of auctions. Here is the illustration of it, using the 2/1GF System, as an example:

South holds in his/her hand four spades and 8 points, and that is enough points to ask North for more precision on his/her hand, implying a particular interest for spades.

The auction starts like this one, where North makes a 1♣ natural opening bid, to which South responds by asking the question: "Do you have four spades in support?"

North	East	South	West
1♣	*Pass*	1♠	

Example 20-1

It is now North's turn to bid.

North	East	South	West
1♣	*Pass*	1♠	*Pass*
Bid?			

Example 20-2

North has to use one of the bids from the list of responses available in the system. Each and every one of the possible bids shows a hand with a specific structure type and point spread.

Before we proceed, let's make some assumptions concerning game/slam point requirements:

We'll use 24 points for 3NT, 25 points for four in a major, 27 points for five in a minor, 30 points for small-slam and 34 points for grand-slam scale—since we all belong to this new breed of highly gifted players, right?

It is not my purpose to address the list of rebids here, but it is a long one. Instead, I will extract from it the three that show 13-17 points, and they are

- 1NT denying four-card support in spades;
- 2♣ also denying four spades in support but showing a long club suit; and
- 2♠ showing four-card support in spades.

If South has fewer than 8 points, no game is in sight for certain, and the best chance is to play the contract at the lowest possible level. If any of these three bids is acceptable, one would convert the answer into a final statement by simply passing. If not, his/her closing statement should be the rebid of NT, club or spade, whichever one will work best or least poorly. North does not have anything to add to that, even if he/she counts 17 points in his/her hand and accepts, by passing, the contract offered by South.

If South has 12 points or more, playing in the game is almost certain. If he/she does not bid game directly, because of being scared of a possible bad distribution of cards, he/she should at least always ask more questions, to make sure there is not a hole somewhere that might make the contract fail. North should not have anything to add to that either and would just accept the contract.

There remains the case in which South has 8-12 points. Game might be possible or not possible, depending on distribution factors. To get a better idea of how high that contract can be played, additional questions must be asked by the captain.

This is where experts excel. They seldom pass on such a point count, as opposed to all the other players who might or might not investigate further.

The only time an expert would pass is if his/her hand had no shape, as with a 4-3-3-3 or 4-4-3-2 distribution. There is no fit in spades, since 1NT denies four-spades support. Even if there is a fit in clubs or diamonds, it requires a higher point count to play in game in minor suits, and it is already established that that point count is not there.

I call this type of point spread *marginal*.

Other types of marginal point spread are the ones that determine the chance of success for playing in a small-slam contract and grand-slam contracts.

A rule of thumb is that one needs to narrow the point spread within four points for a game contract, three points for a small slam contract, and two points for a grand slam.

Further along, I will get to the other factor that is to be considered; that factor is the card distribution.

This was only one example. There are many other combinations of openings/questions/answers that are used (although not an infinite number), depending on the point values and the shape of the hands. Your bidding system should treat them in a case-by-case study; each bidding system being different from the others, I will not review them all here.

The principle in all systems is still the same: Narrow down the value of hands by asking and answering questions until you are ready to make the commitment to play a specific contract.

CHAPTER 21

Bidding Contracts with Interference

Sometimes, figuring out which team has the greatest point count is not straightforward. It requires at least another round of auction to have a sense of it, as in this auction, where both teams use the SAYC system:

North	East	South	West
1♣	*Dbl*	1♠	*2♥*
Bid?			

Example 21-1

The 1♣ shows an opening point count, and so does Dbl; 1♠ implies some points, and so does 2♥.

Regardless of what 1♠ may imply, it is a question by South to North and must be answered.

The answer by North to South's questions should not be influenced by the interference from the other team, unless North's hand is a weak opening hand. In that case, he/she would not have to rebid, since West has placed a bid in between, and South has another chance at asking a new question.

Just en passant, as the French say, some players may use a pass as a rebid to insidiously find out how good the captain's hand really is. This practice must be used with extreme caution. The captain may misinterpret the meaning of that pass, and this might make the auction derail. I personally don't recommend it to any player who is not an expert.

The next round of bidding should determine which team has the advantage in points.

As mentioned earlier, except in the case of a weak opening hand, the rebid by North should not be very different from what it would be without interference.

The only difference is the cueing of the hearts, since hearts was a declared natural suit by the opponents.

A 3♥ rebid by North does not mean 16-21 points with a singleton or a void. It is now showing a limited number of clubs and diamonds and a fairly decent opening that is not necessarily a very strong one. It is actually an attempt to gear South to propose a 3NT contract, provided that South has a stopper in hearts. By making such a bid, North also pre-accepts the notion that South may rebid spades or support clubs. In other words, if you ever make this bid, be ready for a 3♠, a 3NT, or a 4♣ contract. If you opened 1♣ with three small clubs, 3♥ is not a bid to make.

In some situations, if you ask too many questions it gives your opponent a better idea of how to defend the hand, therefore minimizing his/her number of guesses and, subsequently, increasing his/her chance at defeating the contract. It is good for the captain to ask questions, but only the relevant ones.

Gerard's Tip of the Night: About Leads

Nonstandard leads usually show nonstandard hands. Use nonstandard leads with extreme caution.

CHAPTER 22

Interfering with Contract Bidding

To compete or not to compete, that is the question!

I will start with a blunt statement: Don't compete with a trash hand. It never works!

In order to compete, the hand must have some redeeming values. It may be a good point count or a good suit, but it has to have at least one of these.

That being said, there are three reasons why a team would want to compete in an auction:

- in the hope of playing the hand
- to give the partner an idea of what to lead when it is time for the opponents to play their contract
- to be pesky and simply prevent the opponents from finding an easy contract

Being pesky may sound like a fun thing to do, but what do you do if your opponent decides to stop bidding because he/she has detected something wrong in the auction, letting you hang yourself in a contract that you have absolutely no chance to make?

Furthermore, your partner probably won't know what you are doing, believing your bid to be the start of a some redeeming value. start asking questions that result in your climbing up levels in the auction and getting both of you even deeper in trouble.

Draw your own conclusions about what I think of being pesky during auctions.

Giving the partner an idea of how to make the original lead is a good thing. It takes the guess out of defending the hand. In order to be efficient, a bid placed in this frame of mind needs to be placed early in the auction; one reason for this is so that the opponents do not decide to let you play the contract. There are exceptions, one of them being the use of Dbl later in the auction. But then, the Dbl might not be made over a suit that could become the opponent's trump, or they might make the contract—with a bonus on top of it!

The other requirement for efficiency is that the suit overcalled has at least two of the three top honors, AK, AQ, or KQ, if no other top honors exist in some of the other suits. If they do, you may get away with holding two of the four honors in the suit, provided that one of them is the Ace or the King.

There is no point in making an overcall to get a lead from partner in a suit headed by the Queen or a Jack. This will not be successful, on the principle that no more than two cards per suit usually bring in tricks in that suit for the defense, especially in a suit contract. If this is the best you have, simply show it later on during the play of the hand.

Your partner will know your overcall is only a lead director if you do not echo his/her questions with an answer. And, yes, this is consistent with all that preceded this statement. The maker of a lead directing call is always the opener for that side, his/her partner being the captain and the one asking questions.

Finally, competing to get to play the hand is very much the same as what was described earlier in the section relative to bidding with interference. After the second round of auctions, one of the two teams will establish its superiority on points and/or card holding, and if it is the defensive team that shows its dominance, it will become the offensive team, and the other team will become the defensive team.

Let's repeat again that the captain of the competing team has the same privileges and obligations as the captain of the offensive team. It should be obvious, though, that if the offensive team has shown game strength, a new suit by the captain of the competing team will hardly have the same weight as it would if the offensive team showed limited strength. Therefore, in an auction like this one, in SAYC,

North	East	South	West
1♣	1♥	1♠	2♦

Example 22-1

and this one,

North	East	South	West
1♣	1♥	Pass	2♦

Example 22-2

the 2♦ shows dislike for hearts, preference for diamonds, and is forcing—unless North does not pass, of course.

Some 2/1GF versions state differently. They say that 2♦ is not forcing. I advise you to discuss the matter with your partner, but if no special agreement is made, consider this as a forcing bid.

CHAPTER 23

Guidelines for Questions by Captain

When the captain asks a question of his/her crew, these should be meaningful to the crew and should allow the crew to have an idea how to steer the auction, in case there are two or more possible answers.

Here is an example of it in this auction:

North	East	South	West
1♦	*Pass*	1♥	*Pass*
Bid?			

Example 23-1

When North's hand has

North	
♠	QXX
♥	X
♦	AKJXX
♣	QJXX

Example 23-2

North could easily rebid either 2♣ or 1NT.

If North wants to favor a contract play in NT, he/she can bid 1NT. If, on the other hand, he/she thinks there is a better chance in playing in a minor, a 2♣ rebid will do that.

You realize that if North rebids 1NT, it is on the assumption, true or false, that South's question of 1♥ implies that South has at least four hearts in his/her hand.

I cannot think of any system in which 1♥ would not be a question, therefore not forcing. In consequence, I find it unlikely, if not impossible, that South's bid of 1♥ would represent having no hearts at all in the hand. It is like creating a convention "on the fly"; it is also called a *psyche*. The American Contract Bridge League and most other contract bridge associations throughout the world condemn this type of psyche for club and national or regional events, but in international competitions they are allowed.

Experts of the game know how to manage gracefully such situations as they create; most other players don't.

I will not cover the aftermath of such an auction; I just wanted you to know that it exists.

The captain must keep in mind that he/she may give up his/her captainship later on in the auction and that his/her partner may pick up the captainship. If that happens, the new captain needs to have the maximum information possible to in turn make his/her contract proposal.

The captain should ask relevant and useful questions. What good would it do the team if the captain were to ask the number of aces after his/her crew opens 1♥, and he/she herself has a few hearts and a mere opening hand? Asking for aces implies that the captain is contemplating slam, and the answer to his/her question will undoubtedly drive the team into a catastrophic board result.

One frequent error to avoid can be seen in the following example:

North	East	South	West
1♥	*Pass*	1♠	*Pass*
2♠	*Pass*	3♥	*Pass*
Bid?			

Example 23-3

What is North supposed to answer to that 3♥ question?

Is 3♥ showing a bad spade suit with four small spades?

Is 3♥ showing a bad hand and no interest for game?

Is 3♥ an invitation to play in hearts and, if so, at what level, 3 or 4?

Is 3♥ asking North to choose between hearts and spades as trump?

The poor player in North has no idea of how good or how bad the captain's hand may be.

All this is to emphasize that the captain's role is to make the final decision; he/she should not let his/her crew do that.

It is the responsibility of the captain to propose a contract and the level at which to play it.

CHAPTER 24

Guidelines for Answers to Questions

As mentioned earlier, answers to captain questions are not always automatic.

Sometimes, as in the example in the previous chapter, two (or sometimes more) responses are valid responses, though most of the time only one answer is more useful.

If the question asked is artificial and part of a convention, all responses are fairly automatic, but if the question is a natural bid, then a human decision has to be made, and that is function of the personality of the player and his/her playing style.

When you are captain, be tolerant of the fact that your partner might not have sent you in the right direction during auctions. In fact, most successful contracts that do not pay off fail because the auction did not end in the proper spot. During the auctions, the crew selected an answer which was valid but that steered the captain on the wrong route, therefore to the wrong contract.

I am sure that you, a bridge player, have ended in a 3NT contract, making five when a six-clubs contract was "cold" at least once in your life.

The fear of misguiding the captain sometimes triggers another problem, which has to be avoided at all cost. It is to make an *ambiguous* answer.

Here is an auction in the 2/1GF system:

The 2♦ by West, captain of the E/W team, is asking East to bid his/her best major. It implies that West's hand has both majors by five or more cards.

North	East	South	West
1♦	*Pass*	**Pass**	2♦
Pass	2NT		

Example 24-1

Does the 2NT means that East does not have support in any of the majors, or is it asking the captain to make a decision?

My reaction when I'm given this kind of answer is: Why would my partner ask me to make a decision when I am already in the seat that makes the decisions?

I have been burned several times in that situation, because with my luck, I always interpret that the wrong way. But is there a right way?

Only one player at a time may ask a question. The other must answer, not ask a different question.

Captainship in a team cannot overlap. I'll refer to a very famous book that I read when I was a teenager. It is called *The Diary of Major Thompson*, and it was written by Pierre Daninos, a French writer. The opening line of the book is: "The French are a funny race ..."

Now, I can make fun of the French without offending them, since I am French myself.

One of the observations by Major Thompson about the French is that there were at the time forty million of them, and each had his/her own opinion, making a total of forty million opinions. Sounds like a good start for total anarchy to me!

There may only be one captain per team at any given time; that's all there is to it.

It is the responsibility of the crew to answer questions asked by the captain.

Gerard's Tip of the Night: Luck in Bridge

Luck is when your opponents make a mistake and you don't make one yourself.

CHAPTER 25

Organization of the Conversation

Have you ever tried to speak to someone who doesn't hear you? He/she ignores your statements and only wants to make his/her own statements, or answers your questions with questions, or gives answers to questions you never asked. I bet that you have and that it frustrated you.

Just as in any conversation in any language, there has to be, and there is, a specific, structured hierarchy between partners during the auctions. One of them takes command of the auctions—the captain. The captain asks the questions, and his/her crew answers the questions. The captain is the one who eventually makes the final decision with the closing statement.

This may sound very military-like, but because of the auction aspect of the bidding, the number of times each player may place a bid is very limited. Therefore, there is no room for idle statements or repetition of questions and answers.

Here is an auction sample, in the SAYC system:

North	East	South	West
1♣	*Pass*	1♥	*Pass*
2NT	*Pass*	3♦	*Pass*
3♠	*Pass*	3NT	*Pass*
Pass	Pass		

Example 25-1

After North makes the first statement by opening 1♣, South is asking the first question by bidding 1♥, thus establishing him/herself as the captain of the team. From this point on, and until South makes his/her final statement, South will remain the captain and keep asking the questions, which North will have to answer.

Our model would look like this:

North	East	South	West
Active Opening statement Opening bid 1♣	*Passive* *Opening* *statement* *Pass*	**Response** Captain Question 1 1♥	*Response* *Closing* *statement* *Pass*
 Answer 1 2♠	*Pass*	**Captain** Question 2 3♦	*Pass*
 Answer 2 3♠	*Pass*	**Captain** Closing statement 3NT	*Pass*
Accept decision Pass	*Pass*		

Model Extract 25-1

Even I have difficulties reading the chart presented this way.

I will rewrite this example, using a separate column for comments next to each bid where a comment is necessary, and the symbols

O for opening statement,
I for invitation,
Q for question,
A for answer,
C for closing statement,
E for end auction, and
* for captain.

North		East		South		West	
1♣	O	*Pass*	O	1♥	*Q	*Pass*	E
2♠	A	*Pass*		3♦	*Q	*Pass*	
3♠	A	*Pass*		3NT	C	*Pass*	
Pass	E	*Pass*					

Example 25-1

Since the captain is the responder, why would we have two different names to describe the same person?

When any auction starts, the responder is always the captain, as we have already established.

In our example, after North opens with 1♣, his/her partner (South) automatically becomes the captain of the North/South team, because South has more information about North than North has about South.

For the East/West team, there were only an opening statement and a final statement, and the captain in West forfeited his/her right to ask questions and gave up his/her captainship by doing so.

Once the captain has made his/her final decision, which is also a statement, if there is room left in the auction, his/her crew can take over the captainship and, in turn, ask his/her own questions, which the partner will have to answer, as in the extension of the previous example, using the Gerber convention:

North		East		South		West	
1♣	O	*Pass*	O	1♥	*Q	*Pass*	C
2♠	A	*Pass*	E	3♦	*Q	*Pass*	
3♠	A	*Pass*		3NT	C	*Pass*	
4♣	*Q	*Pass*		4♦	A	*Pass*	
5♣	*Q	*Pass*		5♥	A	*Pass*	
7NT	C	*Pass*		Pass	E	*Pass*	

Example 25-2

Contrary to what some players would like to have you believe, 4♣ over any number of NT, in the SAYC and 2/1 systems, is not a natural bid, but a conventional bid that belongs to the Gerber convention. If the Gerber convention is not being used, the bid shows a control in clubs and asks crew to show his/her lowest control available, unless they have a partnership agreement that implies otherwise.

We just saw here a case in which at the end of the auction the captain was no longer the responder, but the opener was. For that reason, we need to separate the concept of captainship from the ones of opener and responder.

CHAPTER 26

Recognizing the Nature of Bids

This chapter is dedicated to determining what your position is in the auction at any given time.

As a function of your position in the auction, your partner's bids will have a different meaning.

It is, therefore, important for you to know at each step of the auction where you stand.

If you are the first one to bid for your team, you will always make an opening statement. It is usually natural, except for an undefined strong hand in most systems, and in specific opening conventions where your first bid does not mean you have that suit. In SAYC and 2/1GF, this would be 2♣; in most strong club systems it would 1♣; in Multi 2D sub system, 2♦, etc.

After you have made your opening statement, either by passing or bidding anything else, the responder, your partner, is the de facto captain. He may ask you questions, to which you must supply answers that truly and faithfully reflect your holding in points and distribution, and he is in charge of making the final statement.

As a general rule, any new suit by the captain is always a question, unless he/she:

- rebids any of his/her own natural suits;
- supports any of your natural suits; or
- bids NT and that NT is not an artificial bid.

Beware that in an auction that starts this way,

North		East		South		West	
Pass	O	*Pass*	O	1♥	*I	*Pass*	C
2♣	A	*Pass*	E	2♦	*Q		

Example 26-1

North has made a passive opening statement, and therefore South's 1♥ opening bid is a question to North. South is the captain for the team.

The 2♣ is the answer by North, denying four cards in hearts and showing a natural clubs suit.

The 2♦ is a new suit (and a new question) by the captain and therefore a question which North must answer, even though there has not been any jump or any opponent's suit cue bid.

Whatever follows in this auction is irrelevant to us right now.

If the captain does not ask a question, his/her bid is deemed to be a final statement and sets the contract. By doing that, he/she also loses his/her captainship.

You, as crew and not captain, in the auction below, have to have very serious reasons to override the captain's decision of playing in 3NT, his/her closing statement. There are situations in which you might find it necessary to do this.

North		East		South		West	
1♣	O	Pass	O	1♥	*Q	Pass	C
2♠	A	Pass	E	3♦	*Q	Pass	
3♠	A	Pass		3NT	C	Pass	
4♣	*Q	Pass		4♦	A	Pass	
5♣	*Q	Pass		5♥	A	Pass	
7NT	C	Pass		Pass	E	Pass	

Example 26-2

Once the captain has made his/her closing statement, the captainship is abandoned, and you, as his/her crew, may pick it up.

The process of questions and answers restarts and continues until a new closing statement is made.

All statements, questions, and answers prior to the final statement of the responder when he was the captain can be used but as informational material only.

Again, as much as the answers you give to the captain's questions must be precise, the captain's questions do not have to feed you information about his/her hand, though it is preferable in situations when the captainship is picked up by the crew—you, in this case.

Staying with our example, let's assume that you were the opener. Once your partner, the captain, had bid 3NT, you might have asked yourself, "Why did he/she ask if I had hearts when making the 1♥ bid, then ask if I had diamonds with the 3♦ question and, finally, settle in a 3NT contract? Could it be that he/she has five hearts and four diamonds?" It is most likely the case. In this auction, after the 3NT closing statement is done, the shape of the hands would look something like this (where *X* represents a card, any card):

YOU			YOUR PARTNER	
♠	XXXXX		♠	XX
♥	X		♥	XXXXX
♦	X		♦	XXXX
♣	XXXXX		♣	XX

Example 26-3

or a variation of this distribution.

Point-wise, you have 16 or more points, and your partner has made a reverse bid, showing an opening hand and placing your team very close to the slam zone.

Re-launching the auction with 4♣ may be courageous, especially with 16-18 points, but it is not outrageous. If the response you get from your partner is not promising, you can always bail out before reaching slam.

Some experts may actually ask questions that are not based on their own hand, in order to either find some fine details of a specific aspect of the crew's hand or to mislead the opposition. In bidding systems like Precision and Italian Blue Club, it is a common thing that has a name: asking bids; but in some other systems it relies exclusively on the creativity of the captain. In these systems, asking bids can only be done when the captain knows for sure that his/her crew will not relaunch the auctions, since the crew would have no valid information about the captain's hand.

Be warned, though, that psychic bids are not overly welcome in most bridge games. They have to be used sparingly, if at all. On top of it, always remember that a psyche may very easily turn against you and haunt you forever.

CHAPTER 27

Integration of External Conventions

A convention is a group of one or several bids allowing, just as do bidding systems, the communication of information, as we saw earlier.

Conventions are not intrinsic parts of bidding systems but are inserted in them, as are the artificial bids we reviewed earlier.

Under the term *convention*, I purposefully include partnership agreements, since the mechanism is the same.

Each convention's purpose is to refine the bidding in a way bidding systems are unable to do, since there is no perfect bidding system. Even the most elaborate bidding systems do, indeed, need refinement in order to improve on the flexibility and efficiency of bridge conversations.

Thousands of conventions have been created and developed, as we mentioned earlier. More are being invented each day. It is difficult to imagine that any system could possibly use all these conventions. For a starter, the system would become too cumbersome and unmanageable. Some of the conventions would clash: Using Flannery 2♦ and Multi 2♦ opening at the same time is impossible, at least until someone takes the time to research how to make that work.

Scholars of the game may wish to use any and all possible conventions, but common sense dictates that if they do not play with other scholars, they are limited to the ones their partners know.

If you know all the conventions ever written, and your partner only knows twelve of them, you will only be able to use these twelve during any game with this specific partner, until you have taught him/her additional ones.

It seems obvious, to me at least, that if during the auctions you come up with an Exclusion Blackwood bid, when your partner has no idea of what it is and has never heard that convention name before, your partnership is heading toward a major catastrophe—not only in the board you are currently playing, but also in the rest of the game. Your partner will feel uneasy about any bid thereafter, fearing that it might contain some question to which he/she does not know the proper answer, and your game will go to hell.

The number-one rule of any partnership in bridge is: **Never make your partner feel inadequate.**

As I also mentioned earlier, you can have the best game and winning game without using any convention at all, provided that you and your partner know your system basics well. The inconvenience is that some auctions may be more convoluted, and the guess factor may be higher than if you were using conventions, but overall, it would not impair your game. In the worst of cases, you might end up in a contract that was not the absolute best contract and therefore miss a "Top," but you would very seldom end up with a "Bottom" because of it.

In a duplicate game, if you succeeded in having averages on most boards, no bottom scores, and good scores on a few boards, you might not win the event, but you would at least earn some master points in any given bridge club.

There are different types of conventions. Some of them are just one bid, the purpose of which is to condense several bids and to start the auction for one team.

A typical example of this is the Flannery Convention.

In SAYC and 2/1 GF (but not limited to these two bidding systems), for instance, with a hand that has four spades and five hearts with eleven HCPs, you would need to make a bid between 1♥ and the bid showing your spade suit (2NT, for instance); otherwise, the responder and captain would believe that you had 17 or more points, would bid accordingly, and would certainly end up in a disastrous contract. See the hand described below:

North			South	
♠	KJ72		♠	T653
♥	AQ985		♥	
♦	J6		♦	AK832
♣	J5		♣	KQ84

Example 27-1

The auction would look like this if you didn't use the Flannery Convention:

North		East		South		West	
1♥	O	*Pass*	O	2♦	*Q	*Pass*	*F
2NT	A	*Pass*		3♣	*Q	*Pass*	
3♠	A	*Pass*		Pass	*F	*Pass*	

Example 27-1A

When the responder and captain, in the SAYC system, responds 2♦, he suggests having 11 or more points with a longer diamond suit than any other suit, and the team would end up in a less-than-cold 3♠ contract because the fit in spades was never found at the two level. The opener could not possibly have bid 2♠ after bidding 1♥ without showing 17 points or more. (This is also called a reverse.)

The Flannery convention states that opening 2♦ describes a hand that contains five hearts, four spades, and between eleven and fifteen HCPs, just what North has in his/her hand. It must be a miracle!

Using the Flannery convention, the auction would now look like this (the star placed after the bids shows bids belonging to the convention):

North		East		South		West	
2♦*	O	*Pass*	O	2♠	*F	*Pass*	*F
Pass		Pass					

Example 27-1B

The 2♠ shows a fit in spade and sets the contract. No questions are asked.

The object of this work is not to teach you the Flannery Convention, but to teach you how it may be used in the context of an auction. For further detail and explanations on the convention, please refer to your book or books of systems or conventions.

Another example of a convention that starts the auction for one team is Michaels. (Please refer to your book or books on systems for complete description of the convention.)

Here is an example using the Michaels Convention. The hands are below:

East			West	
♠	K9872		♠	T653
♥	AQ985		♥	K4
♦	4		♦	AK832
♣	75		♣	Q2

Example 27-2

The auction would look like this:

North		East		South		West	
1♦	O	2♦*	O	Pass	*F	2♠	*F
Pass		Pass					

Example 27-2A

In both conventions given as examples, one bid shows two suits and a limited hand. Other conventions of this type will show two suits, like unusual NT, where,

North		East		South		West	
1♦	O	2NT*	O	Pass	*F	3♣	*F
Pass		Pass		Pass			

Example 27-3

the 2NT shows both lowest unbid suits by five cards or more.

This is not an exhaustive list of this type of convention. Conventions are all alike in that they start the auction for one team, usually limit the hand in points, and show several suits or lack of suits.

Another type of convention is the one embedded within the auction. We already mentioned the most famous one, the Stayman Convention. There are many, many more, and listing them would take forever. They are already the subject of very famous books.

The conventions of the embedded type all have an entry point and an exit point. The entry point is a specific bid.

Here is an example of the use of it:

North		East		South		West	
1NT	O	*Pass*	O	2♣*	*Q	*Pass*	*F
2♥*	A	*Pass*		2NT*	*F	*Pass*	
3♠	*Q	*Pass*		4♠	A	*Pass*	
Pass	*F	*Pass*					

Example 27-4

The 2♣ bid is the entry point of the convention. The captain asks his/her crew whether he/she has a four-card suit or not. The crew answers, "Yes, I have four hearts" and bids 2♥. The captain states, "Forget it. I don't have four hearts, and I only have eight points," and he/she then bids 2NT.

Normally, the auction is over, the captain having made his/her final statement, but in our example, the opener reopens the auction with, "Wait a minute—it is not over yet! I have four spades too, and we have a fit, since you need to have at least one of the majors by four to ask me the question in the first place, and it is not hearts that you have. I am the captain and taking over the auction." He then invites game in spades with a 3♠ bid (denying 17 points in his/her hand).

South, as a good bridge player, reevaluates his/her hand, counting his/her distribution points now that he/she knows that his/her crew has 15 or 16 points, that there is an eight-card fit in spades, and finds one additional point for having a doubleton. His/her conclusion is that a game in spades is a good place to be, and he/she bids 4♠.

The exit of the convention is the rebid by the captain, after he/she has exhausted the list of questions provided to him/her by the convention. In our previous example, there was only one question, and 2NT was the final statement by the captain, thus the end of the use of the convention and the end of the captainship for the responder.

Sometimes exiting a convention does not mean ending the auction. To remain with the Stayman Convention and our example, a rebid of 3♠ by the opener re-launches the auction and sets the opener's captainship. His/her 3♠ is a question to his/her crew meaning: "If you have an extra value in your hand, bid game in spades, or else pass."

This example, as simple as it may be, encapsulates what happens in any and all auctions when a convention and/or a partnership agreement are used.

Let's try another example and make it as complex as possible, using the 2/1GF system, the Multi 2D, Puppet Stayman, and Roman Key Card conventions.

North		East		South		West	
2♦¹	O	*Pass*	O	2♥¹	*Q	*Pass*	*F
2NT¹	A	*Pass*		3♣²	*Q	*Pass*	
3♠²	A	*Pass*		4NT³	*Q	*Pass*	
5♣³	A	*Pass*		5NT³	*Q	*Pass*	
6♥³	A	*Pass*		6♠³	*F	*Pass*	
Pass		Pass					

Example 27-5

In Multi 2D, 2♦ is an artificial opening statement that means that the hand is either the equivalent of a weak two bid for one of the majors or shows 20-21 points and a balanced hand. (I know, I know! Some people use a different hand structure for Multi 2D, but that is the one I will be using in this example).

The 2♥ is a question to the dealer, asking him/her to pass if his/her hand is weak and contains six hearts. As responder, the 2♥ bidder is now the captain for the team and will remain so until he/she has made his/her closing statement.

The 2NT is the response to the 2♥ question and shows a balanced hand with 20-21 points.

The captain could pass at this point, with no or close to no values in his/her hand, and that would be the closing statement that 2NT is an acceptable contract. In our example, he/she selects to bid 3♣ instead, from the Stayman Convention variation called Puppet Stayman. It is a new question and a forcing one, since 3♣ is the entry bid into a convention, an artificial bid.

The 3♠ by the dealer is the response to the Puppet Stayman call of 3♣ that shows five spades.

The captain could have again made a closing statement by bidding 4♠, showing his/her acceptance of spades as trump and of playing at game level, but he/she chose to go further and now bids 4NT, also accepting spades as trump and asking the dealer to show his/her key cards (in Roman Key Cards Convention, they are the four Aces and the King of trump).

We are now inside the third convention call. After the dealer has shown zero or three key cards and two Kings outside of the King of trump, finally, the captain decides to play the contract in 6♠.

All decisions in this auction were made by one person, and one person only—the captain. First he decided to play at a level higher than a partial contract. Then he attempted to play the hand in a major suit by preference over NT. Finally, he selected to attempt a slam.

Even though the dealer had more points than the responder, he was not the captain in this auction and had no power to decide.

All the dealer's answers to the captain's questions were precise and to the point. This is the only way that the captain of a team can reach the right contract and/or the captain of the opposing team can compete efficiently. In any good partnership, it must be so.

Here is a little story that may help you understand this statement.

I needed to go to San Francisco from Los Angeles. My wife had booked the ticket, which contained all the information about the trip. As usual, I was late, and we sprinted to Los Angeles Central Station. She threw at me, "Platform 7!" There was a train there, all right, but it looked more like a suburban train than a train that goes long distances.

I asked her, "Are you sure it's the right one?"

The voice on the loudspeaker screamed, "All aboard!"

She smiled at me and said, "Have a good trip, darling." I had just enough time to step into the car as the train started to move. A few miles and a few minutes later, I realized that I was traveling south instead of north. I had taken the wrong train and missed my destination.

The reason for it was the bad passage of information. The cost of it was time and money.

Bridge auctions are of the same nature. If the captain does not ask the right question at the right time, or his/her crew does not answer or does not answer properly, the final decision as to what contract and what level to play at will be flawed, and he/she will miss the contract.

When using a convention—any convention—make sure that you and your partner are both using the same definition. But this is not enough. Your partner should have a clear idea of why you are using it. Therefore, even if a convention exists, avoid using it when it is not needed.

CONCLUSION

No matter what system you and your partner have selected to play your bridge session, the experience will be much more enjoyable if you understand, assimilate, and apply the concepts I have listed in the earlier chapters.

I have been doing that myself for years, but, to my great regret, I had never found a way nor taken the time to document them until today.

When playing on the Internet, where dozens of spectators may come and watch games in progress, I am always surprised that I attract so many of them.

I suppose that this is because, without understanding my motivations for performing some of my bids, they are intrigued by them and by the results they generate. Sometimes I can hear someone say, "Well, that's a Gerard bid!" but it is all right. Those who understand what the thought process is behind these seemingly strange bids soon stop making such statements.

As I explained in the preceding chapters, the basic idea in bidding is, first, to know who the captain is and who the crew is at any given time during any auction. If you know that, you will know the meaning of the opening statement, what questions and invitations to make, how to answer the questions asked, how to respond to invitations, and what closing statement to make. For each and every one of these, you will ask yourself, "What will my partner understand if I make this particular bid?"

Secondly, when you are the crew you will need to think in different ways than when you are the captain. The crew thinks about what he/she wants to communicate to the captain. That thinking takes place in plain English. Once the crew knows what he/she wants to tell the captain, he/she translates the thought into bridge language (in the form of a bid).

The captain, in turn, listens to the crew's bid (bridge language) and then translates it back into plain English. After analyzing the situation by combining what he/she knows for sure (his/her own hand) with the information received from the crew, the captain decides whether or not more information is needed from the crew before making a decision on the contract to play. If he/she feels that more information is needed, he/she decides then what is required (in plain English) and then translates the question into bridge language (in the form of a bid).

The crew, in turn, will translate back the captain's bid (bridge language) into plain English, and the process starts over again and continues until the captain can make his/her final decision.

That is the way the conversation is carried throughout the auction.

Bridge games, nevertheless, do not end with the auction. The realization of a contract and the defense against a contract are also based on how well the communication between the team members works. I anticipate writing about that subject in the future, since playing contracts and defending against contracts also are part of the concept that *Bridge Is a Conversation*.